A NEWER WORLD

A NEWER WORLD

The Progressive Republican Vision of America

Edited by
REPRESENTATIVE JAMES LEACH
and
WILLIAM P. McKENZIE

MADISON BOOKS
Lanham • New York • London

Library of Congress Cataloging-in-Publication Data

A Newer world : the progressive Republican vision of America / edited
by James Leach and William P. McKenzie.
p. cm.
1. Republican Party (U.S. : 1854–   ). I. Leach, James, 1942–
II. McKenzie, William P. (William Philip), 1954–
JK2356.N48   1988
324.2734—dc 19   88–21529 CIP
ISBN 0–8191–6827–0 (alk. paper)

All Madison Books are produced on acid-free
paper which exceeds the minimum standards set by the National
Historical Publications and Records Commission.

"Come, my friends, 'tis not too late to seek a newer world"
—"Ulysses," Alfred, Lord Tennyson

Contents

ACKNOWLEDGMENTS

Any book of collected essays, particularly one which contains all original work, is the result of hard work by many people. The writing of "A Newer World: The Progressive Republican Vision of America" is no exception. We would like first to thank the authors who have contributed to this book—Ambassador Elliot Richardson, Senators Mark Hatfield and Robert Stafford, Representatives Nancy Johnson and Bill Green, and Ripon Forum contributors Alfred Tate, Steven Klinsky, William Clohan, Donald Bliss and Roman Buhler.

The production of "A Newer World" is also the result of editorial assistance and suggestions by Barry Edwards, Kathy Ceja, Rick Rolfe, Hank Rodin and Vic Merki. Ripon Society President Mark Uncapher provided comments and ideas for this work, and we would like to thank the many Society members, including our past executive director Jayne Hart, who lent their support.

"A Newer World" received strong encouragement from our publisher, James E. Lyons of Madison Books, and from our editor, Charles Lean of Madison Books. Along with the Ripon Society's policy board, our Madison publisher and editor provided welcomed guidance, particularly during the early stages of this work. For that—and the work of everyone listed above—we are grateful.

—James Leach
—William McKenzie

Introduction:
American Values for the 21st Century

Representative James Leach

Every society has a Santayana—an historian who points out that to fail to study the past is to condemn the future to the repetition of past mistakes.

What, for instance, could be more relevant to our understanding of the Nicaragua problem than study of the classics, particularly Thucydides?

Two and a half millennia ago in a chronicle of the Peloponnesian War, Thucydides recorded how the Athenian assembly voted to send ships to conquer the island of Melos, whose people declared they wanted to remain neutral in the great struggle of the Greek age. The day after the fleet was ordered to sail, the assembly reconsidered and a vessel was ordered to convey new orders of restraint. Melos received a reprieve.

Thirty years later the same issue was revisited. This time the order was not reconsidered and Athenian forces landed on Melos, killing the males and enslaving the females of the island.

Thucydides' account was intended to portray the flowering and then the decay of Athenian democracy. Today America stands as the Athens of our time; the Soviet Union, an ideologically more rigid Sparta. The question we must ask ourselves, as our democratic forefathers did 2500 years ago, is whether it is possible to respect the right of a small country to self-determination even if it implies living with a government in our region which articulates a philosophy repugnant to our own.

In a broader historical framework the most challenging assignment for civilization is to figure out how not to make the one mistake that can't be repeated: nuclear Armageddon. What distinguishes this generation of citizens of the world from all others is that we are the first to have the capacity not just to wage war, but to destroy civilization. As Einstein once noted, "The unleashed power of the atom has changed everything save our modes of thinking." If war is a constant of history, the greatest political science question of all time is how it can be made to be obsolete.

Here, the role the imagination plays cannot be underestimated. For practioners of the so-called "art of the possible," the trait most often prized is pragmatism and calculating realism. Yet the realists have brought us an unreal world. It may be that the very stuff of survival demands that the human imagination be stretched in ways it never has before.

In the fast-changing circumstances of the 20th century, a premier responsibility of government is to expand society's commitment to education, with the understanding that the premier responsibility of the education community is to stimulate the imagination, to provide perspective, to enlarge the capacity of the individual to manage change, personal as well as public.

The federal interest in higher education dates back to the founding of our constitutional form of government. Among the proposals under consideration by those who gathered 200 years ago to establish our Constitution was the creation of a national university—an idea whose advocates included, among others, George Washington.

Despite Washington's advocacy, and the good intentions of its proponents, the proposal—presciently—was never adopted. What has evolved instead has been a much more creative public-private sector partnership, punctuated by such milestones as the land grants that gave birth to so many state universities signed by Lincoln at the height of the Civil War. Lincoln's act illustrates the understanding that even in times of trauma civilized society must be prepared to make resource sacrifices to prepare future generations for future leadership.

For the vast majority of recorded history, individuals had only one occupation, that at which their fathers and mothers toiled. Today, young Americans can be expected to have a dozen or two or three jobs. To cope, they will need a good grounding in basic skills and periodic if not continual refining, with education—formal and informal—becoming a lifetime endeavor. Schools are no longer for the young, but for the middle-aged and retired as well. They are for all of us, all the time.

Whatever discipline or disciplines are taught, the key is the manner in which the individual's imagination is stimulated to think and act.

In this context, it is impossible not to be concerned with the state of American ethics.

As evidenced by weekly indictments, the greed syndrome on Wall Street has never been more in evidence. Newsmakers have become those who prey on insider confidences, who manipulate paper rather than grow, invest and build.

As evidenced by the Iran-a-mok episode, the power syndrome in Washington appears increasingly corrupted. White House zealots have ignored common sense in attempting to trade arms for hostages and stretched the law and the Constitution in prosecuting a dubiously moral war in Central America.

As evidenced by the character suicide of a presidential candidate, it appears that some who seek to set an example for American families believe they can ignore traditional family values in their own lifestyles.

And, as evidenced by recent revelations regarding tele-evangelists, moral confidence appears to be shaken not just by those in public life, but by those who by profession have chosen to guide the public, citing the Bible's authority.

Amidst this ethical crisis is a crisis of perspective.

What do these challenges of social ethics embraced in the context of challenges to the survival of the species imply for the individual citizen?

To paraphrase the UNESCO Charter, conflict begins in the hearts and minds of individuals and it is in the hearts and minds of individuals that values must be instilled if society is to be preserved. Responsibility can't be ducked. To sin by silence, by inaction, is to induce moral amnesia.

In our society the Catch-22 of the "me-generation" is what the newly-designated Librarian of Congress, James H. Billington, describes as the growing tendency to decouple freedom from responsibility. Too often modern day conservatives are seeking freedom from government without accepting personal responsibility for societal imperatives. Liberals, on the other hand, are increasingly seeking freedom from personal responsibility by transferring as many problems as possible to impersonal bureaucracies.

The American Revolution was premised on the notion that might did not make right and that self-interest could never be the final measure of an action's worth. Signers of the Declaration of Independence pledged their lives, honors and fortunes to establish a government that constitutionally recognized the separation but not total divorce of church and state.

In crafting our initial documents, our founding fathers attempted not only to imbue our political institutions with an understanding of human nature but with a recognition of the transcendental import of the divine.

Building on the French philosopher Montesquieu, they recognized human frailty and determined that there would be a separation of powers between branches of government with shared and potentially discordant authority. While not establishing a single state church or state school, they nevertheless decreed freedom of religion as a primal right protected by the Constitution itself. Government was to be premised on the active consent of the governed, with the right of revolution against authority, the right of self-determination, rooted in a higher law of conscience as opposed to the lesser, more mundane civil law of society. The government that eventuated—of, by, and for the people—was to be "under," not "above," God.

There is always a tension in a society such as ours that is based on firmly held ethical and religious values but which protects as a fundamental right diversity of perspective. The tension is the genius of our constitutional system. Process is our most important product.

The late Protestant theologian Reinhold Niebuhr once commented that the temper and the integrity with which the political fight is waged is more important for the health of our society than the outcome of any issue.

This emphasis on process as opposed to outcome—the "how" rather than the "who" or the "what" of policy—has never been more important.

The challenge for government in a democracy is to establish laws that deserve respect and for citizens to follow laws even when they find them inconvenient.

But law, to be respected, must constrain the behavior of governments as well as citizens. How the game is played matters . . . as does the temper and integrity of the participants.

World War I taught us how a small event—the assassination of a minor potentate—could spark a global confrontation; World War II taught us how a megalomaniac could not only precipitate a war between states but the genocide of innocents.

Today the greatest threat to world order is the anarchy implied when governments themselves refuse to follow the rules and refuse as well to submit to the kind of arbitration necessary to make law enforceable rather than simply hortatory.

When governments put themselves above the law they invite the retribution of the lawless. And the lawless today are carrying more than six-guns and are motivated by more than the traditional human foibles of greed and gluttony.

Terrorists with access to 21st century weapons rather than bank robbers on horseback should be the greatest concern of Washington policymakers. Yet the type of law and order concerns we too frequently hear trumpeted by politicians apply to the purse snatchers, not the bombardiers.

In an age of ideological, quasi-religious politics, martyrdom—a preference for rather than an aversion to death—is increasingly the norm. It cannot be obviated simply by building nuclear tipped missiles nor by de-mothballing yesteryear's battleships. When a quick entrance to heaven is the goal of potential adversaries, it is imperative that we come to better understand foreign cultures—the Koran as well as Machiavelli—and remember that part of our heritage contained in our first supplication: our revolutionary commitment to pay a decent respect to the opinions of mankind.

In an age of nuclear weapons, the medium truly is the message. When civilization is jeopardized by weapons of mass destruction, detente is not a choice; it is a necessity. Law and order is not a slogan; it is a societal imperative.

Twenty years ago in an address to a small Iowa college a British historian—Arnold Toynbee—sounded an alarm carrying comparable significance to the more celebrated message his fellow countryman—Winston Churchill—delivered fifteen years earlier in Fulton, Missouri.

Churchill warned of an "iron curtain" descending over Eastern Europe. Toynbee spoke of the explosive potential of religious intolerance. Religious dogma interpreted by demagogues, he suggested, could be as dangerous as the secularized convulsion called communism.

Speaking at the height of our civil rights movement, Toynbee chastised Americans for assuming the most profound divisions in the world were based on color of skin. At the same time he chastised the Russians for being so ideologically blind as to believe history could be understood in Marxist economic paradigms. Actually, he predicted, the likeliest causes of conflict in the last half of the twentieth century would be of religious rather than economic or racial derivation. Neither race nor economics, for instance, could explain the Northern Irish problem, Israel's fight for existence, nor the antagonism of India and Pakistan.

One of the most gifted observers of mankind in this century, George Bernard Shaw, said that peace was not only better than war, but infinitely more arduous to achieve. The question that must be asked is: are we learning from the lessons of history and paying attention to the right problems?

For decades there has been debate about whether the United States should play a role of policeman for the world, with some arguing that it is a chore for which we lack either a legal imprimatur or adequate resources to undertake. A new dimension to this debate is implicit in the Reagan administration's policy in Latin America. The administration seems to be suggesting that not only will we play the role of world policeman, but rather than enforcing the law, the interventionist cops American citizens are encouraged to support are themselves above the law. This in the profoundest sense is the meaning of our withdrawal from the compulsory jurisdiction of the World Court because of the case Nicaragua instituted against us.

The most fundamental issues of world politics are, in the first instance, how we contain and constrain weapons of mass destruction and, in the second, how we can best advance the rule of law. To refuse to submit disputes to the World Court and abide by arbitration decisions of that body is to deny our heritage. Today the only real protection against nuclear weapons is an advancement of human understanding and cooperation.

The reality is that the United States will never again claim as great a percentage of the world's economic and military might as it did at the end of World War II. Security in the twentieth century can no longer be unilaterally achieved. It cannot be realized by building walls around our country, turning away from international organizations of cooperation.

In this context, it would appear that both of America's two great political parties are fundamentally letting the country and the world community down.

Two incontrovertible ironies stand out in international politics today. First, at a time when weapons of mass destruction have been developed and allowed to proliferate, individual nation-states have become less rather than more interested in expanding international law and building international institutions, and these nationalistic tendencies are being led by a Republican administration. Second, at a time when the world economy is becoming more interdependent, economic policies within nation-states are becoming more parochial, i.e. protectionist, and this protectionist movement is being led by a Democratic Congress.

The last two centuries have taught us that nationalism is a two-edged sword: it serves to unify people in a constructive and uplifting fashion, often accelerating social progress; but, as two world wars in the first half of this century and as the anarchy and terrorism in the second half illustrate, nationalism can also be perverted by demagogues to tear apart basic human values.

The Reagan administration, while wisely reversing gears on arms control, has tapped irrational nationalistic tendencies and made the world less safe with its interventionist policies, particularly in Central America and with its withdrawal from the full jurisdiction of the World Court. Democrats on the other hand, in espousing economic protectionism, have attempted to tap similar parochial instincts that may be as politically dangerous, if one assumes that economic deprivation is a fundamental cause of war.

While Vietnam hangs as a spectre over the administration's Central American policy, the ghost of Smoot-Hawley haunts the halls of Congress.

National security debates of recent years have shown a Congress willing to criticize a popular president, but unwilling to be held accountable for alternative policies. For liberals the political tradeoff for the military buildup has been the exacting from the Executive of a commitment to maintain a level of social spending far in excess of the curmudgeonly rhetoric of the White House. Somewhat surprisingly, the Great Society's social agenda has been more ensconced than undercut by the most conservative administration of this century.

Hence there is liberal and conservative complicity in the budget deficits, the decision to ask taxpayers tomorrow to pay for today's living standards. Hence also there is shared responsibility for the trade deficit, which, economists suggest, is directly linked (up to two-thirds in magnitude) to the fiscal deficit.

One of the reasons we're confronted with a foreign policy crisis on at least two continents is a failure of leadership in the opposition party, the party that controls Congress. It's amazing how little stomach Democratic leaders have for the real issues of our day. The opposition party in America doesn't understand that when Executive leadership goes astray, it has a responsibility to present alternatives of substantive proportion. But where on a timely basis has the Democratic Party been on the intervention in Lebanon, the savaging of the U.N. system, the torpedoing of the Law of the Sea negotiations, the emasculation of UNESCO, the U.S. withdrawal from the World Court, the administration's rejection of a comprehensive test ban despite, for the first time, Soviet willingness to accept on-site inspection, the Madison Avenue effort to sell a fictitious nuclear umbrella, and, finally, the privatization of the war in Central America?

When all is said and done, the administration has been hypocritical on one of its most important rallying cries—strict construction of the Constitution. To its discredit, the alternative political party has been escapist, failing to focus attention on law and failing to understand that bad economics can drive bad politics. War shouldn't be privatized, nor should its causes. Despite Long Ranger adventurism within the Executive, the administration gets high marks for moving toward free trade zones with Israel, in the Caribbean and with Canada. It is to be commended for pushing new G.A.T.T. rounds, for vetoing textile and other protectionist ploys by Congress.

Centuries hence historians might note that as a society we've experienced three great debates. The first centered around the founding of the Republic and the question of whether a nation-state could be founded premised on the rights of man; the second, symbolized by the Civil War and the Suffragette movement a century later, centered on whether rights would be applied to people who weren't simply male and pale; the third is the debate we're entering today: whether there's a right to peace, whether international stability can be achieved without expanding international law as it applies to trade as well as politics. The outcome of this last debate is unlikely to be happy unless we recognize that law, to be effective, has to constrain the behavior of governments as well as individuals, politicians as well as interest groups.

A Statement of Principles

William P. McKenzie

The coming to power of the conservative wing of the Republican Party in 1980, when Ronald Reagan captured the presidency and six conservative challengers unseated liberal Democratic senators, actually began 25 years before when in 1955 William F. Buckley, Jr. and a variety of conservative writers founded the magazine, *National Review*. Their aim then, as it is now, was to promote a set of principles by which decisionmakers should be led.

Among those principles were a limited government, a strong defense, a hierarchial social order and a reliance upon free markets. And in the ensuing 25 years, conservative Republicans refined, added to, and fiercely promoted those principles. That task resulted in the presidential election of Ronald Reagan, the most conservative president since Calvin Coolidge, if not since the Republic's founding.

Conservative Republicans, however, are not the only members of the GOP with a set of principles. Progressive Republicans also maintain a vision by which decisionmakers can be led. Their ideals include a rational global marketplace, the protection of basic civil liberties, environmental stewardship, an appreciation of decentralized government, an internationalist foreign policy, and a commitment to social justice.

This set of principles is rooted in the early days of the party's founding and can perhaps be best understood when seen in light of what political scientist Everett C. Ladd calls the twin ideas of the "American ideology."

According to Ladd, the first idea is the "national idea," which gives expression to the need for a vital national government. The second idea is the "democratic idea," which rests in the primacy of the individual and is manifested in a distrust of big institutions and central authority. In his work, *The Promise of American Life,* historian Herbert Croly wrote that Abraham Lincoln was the only president to have combined these two ideas. "Lincoln's vision placed every aspect of the [turmoil of the 1850s] in its proper relations," Croly wrote.

At the risk of some chest-thumping, Abraham Lincoln's fusion of the national idea with the democratic idea underlies today's progressive Republican vision. Consider the concept of a vital federal government.

Early Republicans relied upon this idea in their aim to rid the country of slavery in the 1850s. The abolition of that institution demanded a strong federal government to rectify a national problem.

The extension of basic civil liberties over the last two decades has also required the imprimatur of the national government. Ladd made this point when he wrote that those who argued for states' rights during the civil rights battles of the 1960s "failed to appreciate the need for central organization to address needs of the entire nation— where the fulfillment of individualism requires things that political and economic individualism is unable by itself to achieve."

This recognition led such progressive Republican senators as Charles Mathias and the late Jacob Javits to work to ensure that civil rights were afforded blacks and other minorities. According to *Newsweek* columnist Meg Greenfield, who wrote recently about that era: "The principal agitators in town for dramatic civil rights legislation were liberal Republicans."

In the 1980s progressive Republicans also have argued that the federal government must protect basic civil liberties. Senator Lowell Weicker's 1982 filibuster against legislation permitting sectarian prayer in the schools was instrumental in protecting First Amendment freedoms. Likewise, progressive Republicans Mathias and Hamilton Fish, a New York congressman, took action in 1985 to ensure the extension of the Voting Rights Act. They joined then-Senate Majority Leader Robert Dole in filing an amicus brief with the United States Supreme Court to protest an attempt by the Reagan administration to weaken the Voting Rights Act. (The extension of that Act in 1982, which was first passed in 1964, was due largely to the efforts of moderate and progressive Senate Republicans who made it clear to President Reagan that, despite the opposition of some conservatives within his administration, he should sign this legislation.)

New Jersey progressive Republican Governor Thomas Kean also ran for reelection in 1985 on the theme that the promotion of rights is directly related to the creation of opportunity. According to Kean, such programs as affirmative action and minority business quotas are needed to create a level playing field. "The message of dependence, in my experience, is not what the black community wants," Kean said on election night in November 1985. "What they do want is opportunity and they want to make sure that opportunity is there . . . where everybody is going to be at the same place in the starting gate."

New Jersey voters rewarded that message in 1985 by sending Kean back to the governor's mansion with over 75 percent of the popular vote. Black and union voters especially rewarded that message, as over 60 percent of black and union voters supported the incumbent.

Today, of course, rights issues exist in a different context. Washington lawyer Donald Bliss notes this in his chapter in this book when he writes that instead of doing away with obvious inequities, the federal government is now being called upon to reconcile a "clash of rights and values."

The advances in medical technology provide an example. According to Bliss: "The ability to predict diseases based on genetic analysis will create countless opportunities for discrimination in jobs, insurance coverage, and even with respect to such fundamental values as the right to marry and bear children."

The protection of such information, which is related to the right to privacy, will clash with the rights of prospective spouses and unborn children. The rights of the insured to reasonable premiums based on known risks is also at stake, and reaffirms what Bliss says: "Today's debate over AIDS testing is only the tip of the iceberg."

The idea of a vital national government also extends to the progressive Republican commitment to social justice. Throughout this century, the Republican Party has produced some of the nation's most progressive legislation. The GOP was responsible for the Sherman Anti-Trust Act, the Homestead Act, numerous federal conservation statutes, the creation of the Food and Drug Administration and the Department of Labor, child labor laws and the Norris-LaGuardia Act, which limited federal injunctions against labor unions.

Such pieces of legislation were progressive in that they sought to empower individuals to master their own destiny. They were not paternalistic, as some Democratic Party approaches have been. Instead, they were aimed at providing individuals the freedom to make choices about their future.

Another area in which a vital national government is needed is education. Former Undersecretary of Education William Clohan writes in this book that, despite the rhetoric of the conservative movement about abolishing the Department of Education, such an institution is needed. "Education is not now, nor should it be, primarily a federal function," Clohan claims. "However, the federal government does have responsibility for certain facets of education in the United States."

This includes providing financial support for teachers, equipment, books and classrooms that make equal educational opportunities possible. (The federal government usually provides less than ten percent of the financial support for aid to education.) The federal government must also guarantee access to educational opportunities, which includes those with special needs, such as the handicapped.

Not all education issues, however, can or should be solved through the federal government. State and local governments, as well as the private sector, are in a unique position to address such problems as job training.

Consider the Job Training Partnership Act (JTPA), which was created in 1982 to replace the outdated Comprehensive Employment and Training Act (CETA). Unlike CETA, JTPA involves local business people in deciding where federal dollars can be spent for job training. Local business people also decide on what type of training is needed for their area.

Incentives are built into this plan to assure that local job training decisions are made wisely. For example, under JTPA funds are allocated to a university or job trainer based upon whether a JTPA recipient completes his or her coursework and finds a job. According to Clohan, this "performance-based focus" has resulted in higher placement rates and a better cost-benefit to the federal government. (Other incentives that can ensure quality local educational decision-making are matching funds from private sources, performance-based contracting, incentive payments for successful completion of objectives or disincentives when an objective is not met.)

This decentralized approach to decisionmaking is essential to the "democratic idea." The progressive Republican commitment to that concept, which reflects a distrust of overly-centralized institutions, was reflected in a proposal put forth in 1983 by Republican Senator John Heinz to promote neighborhood development. The Heinz plan, which Congress adopted in 1983, provides federal matching funds to neighborhood development organizations. The level of those funds is based upon the amount of money an organization can raise from local institutions. And the federal dollar is unattached so that a neighborhood development organization can best determine how to create new jobs, stimulate business development, improve vocational training, and provide neighborhood clean-up and protection services.

In 1972 Richard Nixon embraced the same concept when he signed into law general revenue sharing. Originally promoted by Republican Congressman Melvin Laird, revenue sharing was designed to provide state and local governments with the flexibility to solve their own problems. The federal government raised the money through income taxes, but passed it back to the states through open-ended grants. The only significant provisions were that states could spend their funds for "normal and customary use," while localities had to spend their funds for "necessary and ordinary capital" expenditures, or "priority expenditures." The latter included public safety and transportation, environmental protection, health and hospitals, and social services for the poor and aged.

In this book the problem of overly-centralized authority is addressed by Elliot Richardson, who has held five Cabinet positions and written widely on the subject of governmental structure. In his essay, Richardson writes:

> "In a book written more than ten years ago, I argued that the federal government was already confronted by excessive demands. The resulting tendency toward top-heaviness, intrusiveness, and remoteness from popular understanding and control had to be resisted. Any new program, therefore, should be required to sustain a heavy burden of justification. . . . All this is even clearer now. Today's challenge is to keep the federal government from being totally overwhelmed by the additional tasks that no other level of government is equipped to perform."

To resolve that conflict requires an improvement in the nation's civil service. In part, this stems from executive leadership. Instead of "bashing" Washington, our next leader should address the need for a more experienced, less political, and better paid civil service. The diversity of the nation's problems will require greater creativity, which is directly related to the motivation of federal decisionmakers. The intrusiveness of government into our daily lives has already gone, as Richardson says, "disturbingly far." The success of managing that intrusiveness depends on the ability of those who direct government programs.

The synthesis of Ladd's "national idea" with the "democratic idea" is particularly evident in the progressive Republican commitment to a rational global marketplace and to individual economic freedom. New York investment banker and Ripon editor Steven Klinsky writes in "Untying the Knot: The Economics of Honesty" that the federal government is:

> ". . . neither an omnipotent Great Society saviour nor a supply-side villain. The role of the government is to repair and preserve our fundamental social institutions; to stabilize and improve the overarching forces which buffet us so that individuals can pursue their own lives and goals in the most fruitful possible circumstances."

In its "national" role, the government can best address our chronic budget and trade deficits by correcting the root structural imbalances that create them. First, the government must address the costly and now unjustified disparity in allied defense spending which results in the U.S. paying over 6% of its Gross National Product (GNP) on free world defense while Europe's NATO nations spend under 4% of their GNP and Japan spends a mere 1%. Second, the government must end the instability of the dollar which has caused the interest rate on America's $2.3 trillion national debt to climb to almost twice traditional levels and more than twice current Japanese levels. As Klinsky writes, the budget deficit is not a "question of guns vs. butter. In fact, it is a question of guns vs. butter vs. interest, and if guns, whose guns." Fairer defense spending reimbursement from our allies and a return to traditional interest rates would have more than eliminated even our largest past aggregate budget and trade deficits.

In its "democratic" role, progressive economic policy believes that the government should champion free markets and individual economic liberty. It opposes protectionism against honest foreign competitors as financially destructive and unfair, and rejects quick fix tax increases as unjustified and recessionary. Reflecting longstanding social concerns, progressive Republicans would replace supply-side's "trickle down" economics with a direct attack on the most severe structural poverty. The end result of these ideas is a distinct progressive economic approach: more market-oriented than Democratic Party proposals, more global in orientation than the traditional Republican approach, and more socially progressive than current supply-side thinking.

An understanding of global economics must also extend to an understanding of global politics. In particular, progressive Republicans maintain that modern American foreign policy must be internationalist in scope. This means strengthening international institutions such as the United Nations and preserving the integrity of tribunals like the World Court. This also means being aggressive in "waging peace" through assisting Third World nations in their economic development, expanding international exchanges with such adversarial nations as the Soviet Union, and maintaining open markets with such nations as Japan and South Korea.

Progressive Republicans contend that the process of international dialogue is itself a valuable component of international relations. Although not an exciting phenomenon, nor a headline-grabbing aspect of foreign relations, dialogue is as essential to international order as is maintaining an appropriate military posture.

To be sure, dialogue with other nations involves a great amount of patience. Non-aligned nations in institutions such as the United Nations often love to "blame America first." But to respond with rhetoric about getting the "United States out of the United Nations and the United Nations out of the United States," as some archconservatives have demanded, is misguided. It ignores the deep search for peace that must accompany foreign relations.

Consider the record of Theodore Roosevelt, the great progressive Republican president of the early 20th century. The popular image of Roosevelt is that of a gunboat diplomat. But during the nearly eight years of his presidency, not one soldier or sailor was ever ordered to fire a shot at a foreign foe. Roosevelt signed 24 arbitration treaties and became the first world leader to submit an international dispute involving his own country to the Hague Court of Arbitration. Historian Federick Marks has written of him: "He never believed that peace could be had by sitting impassively behind a wall of battleships. On the contrary. One had to exhaust the full range of expedients, all the way from international tribunals to multilateral conferences, to the subtlest and most adroit diplomacy on a one-to-one basis. It is here perhaps that we discover the meaning of the phrase 'speak softly.' "

Of course, speaking softly must be matched by a well-reasoned defense policy. This includes being specific about America's strategic interests and conventional capabilities. The latter aspect is especially important since the Intermediate Nuclear Force Treaty signed last December by President Reagan and General Secretary Gorbachev eliminates an entire class of nuclear weapons from the European continent. The United States and its NATO allies must now determine the kind of conventional forces that will be necessary to deter Warsaw Pact nations, in particular the Soviet Union, from considering a conventional attack on Western Europe.

Any debate over the United States' conventional capabilities must have as a focus the strategies by which such forces would be used. As an example, the military reform movement, led by progressive Republican Senator William Cohen of Maine and others, has emphasized the need to replace the doctrine of attrition with a plan for "maneuverability."

The strategy of attrition emphasizes heavy weaponry and seemingly endless supply lines to wear down one's enemy. Although that concept worked well during World Wars I and II, it proved inadequate in Vietnam due to the countless number of Viet Cong soldiers, their own seemingly endless supply lines, the futile search and destroy missions conducted by the United States, and, as author James Fallows wrote in his book *National Defense*, "the repeated attempts to draw the enemy into 'decisive' battles.' "

Military reformers emphasize a plan of "maneuverability," which draws heavily upon the philosophy of the ancient military theoretician Sun Tzu. This fourth century B.C. philosopher wrote that the best way to conquer an enemy is to destroy his mind, then make his alliances unstable. Stressing speed, surprise and flexibility, the doctrine of maneuverability is much like an invasion of weaker red ants who capture their stronger prey by pesty, unpredictable strikes.

Maneuverability and flexibility, of course, are not complete answers to our defense needs. But they do provide a start toward determining how the United States can achieve an efficient and effective military posture. They also reflect an awareness of the interdependence of Western nations by making greater use of the defense capabilities of NATO allies. This means relying on Norway's Air Force, which has the potential to intercept Soviet missiles, and Canada's new nuclear submarines, which will patrol Arctic waters.

Internationalism is an important component of the progressive Republican philosophy. It recognizes the reality of the modern world in which global business transactions occur daily, free nations rely upon one another for military support, and Third World countries demand First World assistance. More important, international cooperation is needed to counter the threat to civilization posed by nuclear arms. As Representative Jim Leach writes, "The most challenging assignment for civilization is to figure out how not to make the one mistake that can't be repeated: nuclear Armageddon."

Beyond the Containment Doctrine

Senator Mark O. Hatfield

Well before the Russian revolution stunned the Western world, one of the truly great observers of human nature and government, Alexis de Tocqueville, penned the following words:

> "There are now two great nations in the world: the Russians and the Anglo-Americans. . . . All other peoples seem to have nearly reached their natural limits and to need nothing but to preserve them; but these two are growing . . . America's conquests are made with the plowshare, Russia's with the sword. To attain their aims, the former gives free scope to the unguided strength and common sense of individuals. The latter in a sense concentrates the whole power of society in one man. One has freedom as the principal means of action; the other has servitude. Nevertheless, each seems called by some secret design of Providence one day to hold in its hands the destinies of half the world."

De Tocqueville's observations in the nineteenth century dealt with Russians in a pre-communist era. Yet the accuracy of his perspective on the comparative national character of the Americans and the Soviets rings as true today as it did when he first rendered it. As the Reagan administration comes to a close and a new administration begins, it is useful to assess how far the superpowers have come in the context of de Tocqueville's vision.

The Reagan administration is not one to miss an opportunity to make a point with a picture or an image. There is a map of the world

11

they once gave to me at a meeting of the congressional leadership at the White House. It categorizes the nations of the world by colors. The communist nations are, of course, red. The free nations are brown. And the nations which have become free under the geopolitical guidance of President Reagan are green. There are a lot of green countries on that White House map.

The obvious message is that any recent setbacks suffered by communism or victories enjoyed by democracy have not been a coincidence. In the Machiavellian zero-sum world in which a Soviet loss is our gain, the trend clearly favors the United States. The map is a not so subtle way of attempting to ensure that history does not record as an accident the fact that it has occurred under President Reagan's watch.

Enduring policies have a way of evolving out of simplistic assumptions; and the simpler the better. That "peace through strength" has guided us safely through treacherous waters in the 1980s is an assumption which deserves careful scrutiny. "Strength," in this case, is essentially a professed willingness to use force, a commitment to military superiority and a theory of negotiation which holds that your opponent can only be persuaded by intimidation. Yet if you examine the effectiveness of the three pillars of our current foreign policy, we have not done as well as it would appear.

Even so, the diminishing potency of Soviet communism is an unmistakable and fundamental geopolitical reality of our time. As we observe the internal changes now taking place within the Soviet Union and Eastern Europe, it would be hard to conclude otherwise. Certainly we have not seen communist parties ascend within established democracies. And where communism had made any advances, as in the case of Nicaragua, its purity and its allegiance to the Soviet Union is highly debatable. The salient question is whether a causal relationship can be drawn linking these facts to the Reagan doctrine.

Of the countries which have gone democratic over the last eight years, we cannot really take credit for any of them. It was the Arias peace plan, not force, which brought about the truce in Nicaragua. And it was the Soviet acceptance of on-site verification, a principle our negotiators routinely used to thwart arms control agreements, which broke the logjam in the INF negotiations.

Then there are the problems this administration leaves as its legacy because it deliberately chose not to negotiate them away: nerve gas, underground nuclear weapons testing and the arms race in space are primary examples. Each represents a common danger we chose to embrace rather than eliminate even though its elimination was probably negotiable. With the exception of the INF Treaty, there is very little the U.S. can point to recently in the field of diplomacy with pride. So instead we have created a scoring system which records Soviet losses as American gains and conveniently omits a credible assessment of our own accomplishments. It is an unhealthy exercise in self-deception. It also is a skillful marketing effort to make something very old look new.

The Reagan doctrine is an extension of the principle of "containment" which emanated out of the post World War II period. That thesis, advanced anonymously by Ambassador George Kennan in his famous *Mr. X* article in 1947, held that we must confront the Soviets with counterforce at every point where they threaten a peaceful and stable world. The distinguishing feature of the current administration's version of the containment doctrine is the tenacity and bravado they have brought to an old task.

George Kennan was not oblivious to the very real Soviet military threat in the aftermath of World War II. In fact, he took it very seriously. He was, however, more concerned on the bottom line with the *ideological* appeal of Soviet communism to a civilized world which lay in ruins. He lived to see that concern exploited and distorted as a justification for cold war militarism. It was a good doctrine put to bad use. We risk today a reverse application—a skewed and antiquated containment doctrine touted as a miracle cure for eliminating the disease of communism. The danger lies with the American ego; because it will probably want to believe that it is true.

For better or worse, and for the most part it is better, we Americans cannot escape our national ego. It tells us a lot about why we have held ourselves hostage to the burden of leading the free world. That the Soviet communist score on the card has not fared terribly well over the last decade gives that ego a considerable boost. But it does something else: it diverts us from looking critically at our own score. Over the long run, nothing could be more perilous from a cold, pragmatic national security standpoint.

Throughout the post World War II period we Americans played a multitude of roles on the global stage. We symbolized ingenuity which increasingly became technology. We symbolized the free spirit of humankind. We symbolized compassion for people in need. Depending on where you sat in the global audience, for most of the world—one or more of these attributes represented America and Americanism.

Take them one by one. The fact is that from the standpoint of materialism alone, what had been a uniquely American role on the global stage is not now ours alone to play. Our technology and thus our ingenuity has since been dispersed, transferred, intercepted and diluted. What was once our exclusive domain will forever be shared among many actors. We are no longer and can no longer be the singular global guru of materialism. It is partly our fault, but it is also the result of a natural flow of ideas. No nation can forever lock within its own borders an idea.

As to the symbol of the free spirit of humankind? Go into a major hotel in one of the economic zones in China and you will see dozens, perhaps hundreds of Chinese mesmerized by "Miami Vice" on a giant video screen—watching us roaring around in sports cars shooting at each other. There isn't a foreign newspaper in the world that doesn't enjoy placing our pathetic crime statistics and stories of one-man anti-crime vigilantes on the front page. Shoot first—ask questions later—that is unfortunately becoming the common interpretation of the American free spirit. This interpretation is not only applicable in the context of our domestic life, it describes U.S. policy in the Persian Gulf and Nicaragua. It's embodied in our first-strike nuclear weapons.

As for compassion, we now rank 18th among the nations of the world in our commitment to human need and advancement in the developing world. Global poverty is the contemporary U.S. national security equivalent of the needs of Europe and Japan following World War II. We responded then with foresight and vigor, perceiving clearly the relationship between human need and the advancement of our own national security interests. The federal government does not place a national security priority on combating today's human and economic devastation.

"The numbers stand in long rows," writes Ruth Sivard, "like tombstones, monuments to lives lost to neglect: 100 million people have no shelter whatsoever, 770 million do not get enough food for an active working life, 500 million suffer from iron-deficiency anemia, 1.3 billion do not have safe water to drink, 800 million live in absolute poverty, 880 million adults cannot read or write, 10 million babies are born malnourished every year and 14 million children die of hunger." Yet it is as though a memorandum had been submitted to the president describing this assault on humanity and concluding "hopelessly unmanageable—little progress can be made in one term or even two—recommend extremely low priority attention."

The fact is that our preference for immediate gratification over long-term investment is as pertinent to our crises of global influence as it is to the current American economic crises.

We build weapon upon weapon, ignoring the fact that an investment in arms control could obviate the need for more.

We emphasize military means in response to political and social conflicts, when an investment in combating the root causes of discontent is the only real insurance policy against the threat of revolution.

We manipulate frail allies to keep them temporarily afloat while ignoring the investments necessary to sustain them as true democracies.

We conduct, in short, a "live for today" foreign policy, just as we do in the economic sphere.

You can cut through all the erudite terminology and describe what has been slipping away in one or two words. One would be influence. The other respect.

I don't think the current administration would take issue with the view that it all boils down to respect. And though it would assert that "America is back and standing tall," as the saying goes, the hard fact is that we have a lot less respect than we did 30 or 40 years ago.

In the eyes of this administration and probably a majority in the Congress, respect is measured exclusively by the blood pressure of Soviet generals. Yet global respect and influence aren't simple matters of the blood pressure of Soviet generals. International respect is more profoundly influenced by whether you have a sufficient reserve of technological genius after your defense needs have been met:

- by whether there is enough left over to combat cancer and AIDS;

- by whether there is enough left over to train the next generation to compete in the international market place;

- by whether there is enough left over to devise means and systems by which to provide the world's poor, including our own poor, with food, sanitation, medicine and clean water.

Global respect and influence also depend on whether there is a rational cost-benefit analysis undergirding your foreign policy. Any discussion of cost-benefit analysis in American foreign policy would not be complete without considering the geopolitical equivalent of the cliche: "the tail wagging the dog." If we were to create a graph which assessed national security priorities and measured time, energy, money and prestige—against the degree of success achieved from those efforts: the most glaring failure not only of President Reagan's foreign policy, but of every president's foreign policy since Eisenhower would be our inability to contain Fidel Castro. More often than not, the operative phrase used when assessing the threats we must contain isn't Soviet communism, it is Soviet-Cuban communism.

Fidel Castro is the ultimate living testament to the limitations of the power of a great nation. The Soviets now provide Castro over 4 billion dollars per year to maintain a piece of real estate 90 miles from Florida. That is approximately the amount we provide yearly to Puerto Rico and a fraction of what we expend coping with Castro's hemispheric mischief. Presiding over a population of ten million people; a land mass measuring roughly 44,000 square miles, and wholly dependent on Soviet economic and military support: he exercises global influence totally out of proportion to any logical calculation. He is truly the "mouse that roared."

The focus on Castro usually deteriorates into a debate as to whether he really was a communist at the time of the Cuban revolution or whether our hostility forced him into becoming one. That debate is a distraction from the task of determining the optional course for advancing U.S. national security interests. In all likelihood, Castro's revolutionary fervor was of such a degree that it probably would not have permitted an accommodation between us. He promised to ignite a revolutionary inferno throughout Latin America. And the totalitarian excesses of his regime with its prisons and executions and labor camps were an affront to anyone concerned about human dignity and human rights.

There is a saying in Latin America: "Latin Americans never forget, and the North Americans never remember." We clearly would rather not remember that under the containment doctrine Cuban influence and Cuban prestige has increased in Latin America while ours has diminished. To be sure, one of the reasons most nations in Latin America maintain healthy relations with Cuba is to avoid Fidel Castro's wrath. They are intimidated by him. But more importantly, it is a matter of practicality. In all likelihood, no enduring solution to the conflicts in Central America is possible without Castro's involvement.

In the early days of the Reagan administration we threatened to "go to the source" in an obvious reference to Fidel Castro and his support for Nicaragua and the guerrillas in El Salvador. Yet even before that pronouncement, we had exercised just about every option available—assassination plots, an embargo, an invasion—virtually everything under the sun except bombing Cuba out of existence. Through it all, Fidel Castro emerged the winner. The Reagan administration ratcheted the tension up another notch. This time, they said, no option was beyond consideration. Yet, in the final analysis, with the exception of Grenada, the emotive desire to confront Castro had to give way to the reality that there is no effective way to do it.

To paraphrase President Reagan, we cannot expect to exert influence around the globe if we are failing in our own backyard. True enough. This is a compelling reason to take note of the fact that Castro may well be ready to deal. It appears that he played a constructive role in encouraging the Sandinistas to accept the Arias peace plan. He has indicated through channels that he is prepared to engage in dialogue without conditions with the United States on a range of issues. He is beginning to demonstrate some sensitivity to his human rights image. We can fully expect him to continue to fuel the conflict in El Salvador and to exploit opportunities as they arise, as in the case of Panama. Yet the total picture represents an appreciable change from the days when he vowed to set Latin America ablaze.

It is time to resurrect the Reagan proposal to "go to the source." But this time it should be through negotiation rather than confrontation. There should be no illusion that negotiating with Castro will be a picnic. His global prestige is due to the fact that he can make the most powerful nation in the world squirm, and he will not relinquish that role easily. But if there is an umbilical cord that runs from Moscow through Havana to Managua, we had better get about the business of severing it, or at least altering it.

The reaction one can readily anticipate to this proposal is: "Do you really think you can convert Fidel Castro into a card-carrying capitalist and an ally of the United States?" No, I do not—no more than I think Mr. Gorbachev will disavow Lenin. At least not right away.

Mao died a communist—but that doesn't make President Nixon's undertaking any less rational or successful. Tito died a communist—but we benefited immensely from President Truman's contact with him. Conversion is not the objective—advancing the best interests of the U.S. is.

Observe the miraculous diminution of xenophobia toward the "red" Chinese. Remember that "red" menace? We moved from a level of hate and fear equivalent to that which is now directed toward Fidel Castro to the current relationship almost overnight. Two years before Nixon went to China, the notion that he would come to an understanding with Mao would have been bizarre. Today it seems bizarre that we didn't do it sooner.

With all the criticism one can level at the execution of U.S. foreign policy toward Cuba we at least know who we are confronting and why. There is a rational policy determinant even if the methodology has been proven useless. An interesting contrast can be found in U.S. policy toward the Persian Gulf.

If one were to search for a title to describe U.S. policy in the Persian Gulf today a good one would probably be: "in search of rational policy determinants: no where to be found." The president of the United States, after having been exposed for selling arms to Iran, couched his announcement of the Kuwait reflagging policy in terms of preventing Soviet "control of the Gulf" and Iranian control over "use of the sea lanes." Yet the Soviets had only leased three ships to Kuwait. And Iraq, not Iran, had attacked the U.S.S. Stark and has always been the driving force behind the tanker war in the Gulf. The Defense Department continues to clamor for "vocal" and "visible" support of U.S. policy from Arab states in utter disregard for the internal stability problem this creates for Gulf leaders. Less dangerous options, such as a multilateral peace keeping force in which non-belligerents could fly the U.N. flag were rejected out of hand.

The amazing thing is that this policy evolved against a backdrop of unique geopolitical opportunity. A profound historical shift had taken place in the Gulf states: Iran had displaced Israel as the primary obsession of their foreign policies. If you were to consult with Gulf leaders as to the order of the threats they perceive today Iran would rank first, the Israeli lobby in the U.S. second and Israel itself probably third. In effect, the United States is in an excellent position to advance a diplomatic quid pro quo. We could be working with the Soviets to more effectively engage the U.N. in an effort to end the Iran-Iraq war and stabilize the Gulf in exchange for tangible commitments from Gulf states to address Israeli security concerns.

Addressing the Soviet diplomatic assault underway in the Gulf, George Ball noted the irony of our policy given the unique convergence of superpower objectives there and asked:

> "Does it make sense for our country to try to maintain an exclusive sphere of influence in the Middle East—7,000 miles away from our shores and only 600 miles from the Soviet Union? . . . Would we not be better advised to seize the rare chance presented by the current overlapping of interests

to engage the Soviet Union in a common effort to resolve some of the festering problems that make sleepless nights for each superpower?"

Instead, we have chosen to shatter the windows of geopolitical opportunity and opt for the Iranian "crazy state" approach. When the president said "we want the Iranians to go to bed every night wondering what we might do" he sounded like he was in a rhetoric tournament with Ayatollah Khomeni. At that moment we inadvertently turned the policy initiative over to the very "terrorists" we deplore with the only possible objective being that of determining whether martyrdom imperatives or national survival imperatives would ultimately prevail if Iran is sufficiently provoked. That is not a rational policy determinant.

Having explored two dimensions of a rationality in foreign policy, i.e., that it should be based upon sound cost-benefit calculations and that it should be undergirded by a clear sense of purpose, it is fitting to assess the degree of rationality we bring to bear on the most critical foreign policy issue of all: arms control.

If there were ever a sign that the time-worn Soviet stereotypes are a misleading guide to understanding contemporary Soviet policies, the irrefutable evidence lies with the verification component of the current INF agreement. If one polled virtually every professor teaching at our top international graduate schools five years ago to determine if on-site inspection was a realistic near-term goal of arms control, the response would have been overwhelmingly negative. The Soviets called our bluff on verification and the circumstances were such that we couldn't wiggle out of it. I think history will show that the primary American ingredients in the formula which produced the INF treaty were the following: (1) a sincere desire on the president's part to obtain an agreement; (2) a profound miscalculation on the part of his resident arms control saboteurs that on-site inspection would never be accepted; (3) a sufficient number of rational presidential advisors such as George Shultz and George Bush to seize the opportunity and (4) a First Lady with a grasp of history. The primary Soviet ingredients were its economy and Mr. Gorbachev's courage and vision.

But it is well worth asking the question: should a treaty coming at the end of a two-term administration which does not even address problems of nuclear weapons technology be worthy of support? Underground nuclear testing, plutonium production, nuclear flight testing and the militarization of space remain the high priority targets of honest advocates of arms control. It is the technological dimension, not numbers of weapons, which remain the true lifeblood of the nuclear arms race. If we continue to skirt the fundamental driving forces of the arms race we are in effect building a superpower prison for future arms control negotiators. No matter how hard they try or how much sheer will they bring to the task, we are fast approaching the point where technology may overwhelm best intentions of national leaders. We will be slaves to technology and there will be no means of escape.

Still the only responsible course is to stand firmly in support of the agreement. We cannot risk extending the legacy of arms control wreckage which preceded this agreement into the next administration. The INF agreement is not for President Reagan, it is for the next president. Its principle benefit is to deny a future cadre of arms control saboteurs a breeding ground for its tactics of fear and distortion. If we can make an on-site inspection regime work, it will prove far more difficult for any president or Congress to skirt the fundamental issue of the survival of the human race. This prospect frightens a good number of my Senate colleagues.

CONCLUSION

The fight against communism demands that we break free of the intellectual timidity and laziness which characterize a foreign policy locked in a time capsule. The threat which faced Europe in the aftermath of the Second World War is no longer a valid cornerstone upon which to formulate U.S. foreign policy. The fight is not on the battle lines of Western Europe. The fight is on the front line of global poverty—where guerrillas are created every day who are either too young or too poor to have ever read Marx or Lenin. They emerge from the vacuum of creative geopolitical diplomacy which is created by our reliance on the containment doctrine. And they emerge from our indifference and our inability to see the long range value of investing in people.

A vast discrepancy exists between what the American people have been led to believe about the amount of money and the degree of commitment we extend to a world in need and what we really do. It all adds up to a rather confusing picture for the average American. Ingratitude and terrorism are juxtaposed in the national psyche against images of unlimited benevolence on the part of the U.S. We don't want to see the true picture. We keep one eye on the Soviet score and the other eye closed. It's time to see the world with both eyes wide open.

We've taken to playing semantics games just as we did in Vietnam when we twisted the Food for Peace program into Food for War. In El Salvador we pulverize villages suspected of harboring guerrillas, bring the acceptable people back, let them build tiny homes in the rubble and then call it development. Most of the foreign aid apparatus of this nation has been co-opted, compromised or enlisted in the service of national security charades such as this. There are no micro-strategies or macro-strategies for honest leadership in addressing the growing crisis of global poverty.

What Charles DeGaulle said once of the French, that they cannot be their "true selves unless engaged in a great enterprise," is as true if not truer of us Americans in our global relations. But we cannot embark on that great global enterprise with the myopia we call containment.

We need to be tough because this is a rough and tumble world. But we need to be smart-tough, not dumb-tough. We need to contain the Soviets, yes, but more importantly we need to contain everything which threatens a stable and peaceful world. Many of the things we need to contain threaten the Soviets as much as they threaten us. We must go to the source of global poverty; to the source of revolutions; to the source of communist appeal and adventurism. We need to go to the source in all things instead of dancing around it because the old music makes us feel secure.

Most important of all, we must go to the source of our own greatness. That requires the courage to look in the mirror and see ourselves as we are perceived by others. It is the same with individuals as it is with nations: you are what you do, not what you say you are. We must choose what kind of superpower we want to be and get on with it.

Untying the Knot:
The Economics of Honesty

Steven B. Klinsky

Twenty years ago, British Prime Minister Lord Home remarked that he faced two kinds of problems. The political were insoluable. The economic, incomprehensible.

The progressive Republican vision holds that today's economic problems can be chiefly understood as symptoms of larger institutional factors. It further holds that once these problems are understood, strong leadership can effect a political solution for the long term benefit of all.

First among these factors is the overallocation of the free world's defense burden onto the United States. The security of the West is indivisible and the economic capabilities of America, Europe and Japan are increasingly equal. Yet, America now spends over 6% of its GNP on the common defense while Europe spends under 4% and Japan spends only 1%. This inequity contributes greatly to the current U.S. budget and trade deficits. The remedy of this misallocation, not destructive protectionism, should be the centerpiece of America's allied diplomacy.

The second key factor is the fractured international currency system. The unpredictable rise and fall of the dollar has crippled American competitiveness and raised American interest rates. As of June 1988, the interest rate on long term U.S. government bonds was almost twice the traditional American level and approximately twice the Japanese level. Such extra interest cost on America's $2.4 trillion national debt is a second major—and totally unproductive—cause of our budget and trade problems.

Despite these difficulties and the foreboding omen of the October 1987 stock market crash, by using foreign loans the American economy has performed well under President Reagan. Unemployment has declined steadily and more than fourteen million new jobs have been created since the end of the 1982 recession. Continued economic growth and a demographic-based decline in new job seekers should improve the employment outlook even more in future years. However, the nation must strengthen its educational system so that the coming workforce will be able to fill the job opportunities awaiting them. Educational and family law reforms and a better mix of government programs are needed to combat poverty. False solutions—such as trade warfare, mercantile currency devaluations and government "industrial policy"—must be scrupulously avoided.

In a real sense, the answer to our current problems is an economics of honesty: a financially honest dollar that holds a constant and predictable value against real goods and other currencies; a geopolitically honest allocation of burdens among free world nations based on their current ability to pay; and an intellectually honest conviction to compete hard but fairly within the rules of a free and open marketplace. All such policies must be joined with a moral honesty, recognizing that the battle against the most severe structural poverty cannot be left to free market forces alone.

This essay will begin with an analysis of political economics: a catalog of our current economic ills (real or alleged), the structural imperfections which create them and the political actions required for their solution. It will conclude with an analysis of economic politics: the importance of economic policy to a political party's success, the relation of the progressive economic vision to the broader progressive philosophy and a comparison of the progressive Republican economic approach with competing approaches.

In the progressive view, government is neither an omnipotent Great Society savior nor a supply-side villain. The role of the government is to repair and preserve our fundamental social institutions; to stabilize and improve the overarching forces which buffet us so that individuals can pursue their own lives and goals in the most fruitful possible circumstances. We must address our problems squarely, correct them at the root, and progress.

POLITICAL ECONOMICS: PROBLEMS AND DIRECTIONS

The Budget Deficit

The budget deficit—that traditionally preeminent Republican concern—is generally characterized as a question of guns vs. butter. In fact, it is a question of guns vs. butter vs. interest, and if guns, whose guns.

In the record deficit year of 1986, federal budget expenditures totalled $990 billion while federal receipts totalled $769 billion. This disparity produced a federal budget shortfall of $221 billion, equal to 5.3% of America's gross national product. A surplus in state and local government budgets lowered the aggregate government deficit to $143 billion, or 3.4% of GNP.

The federal expenditure consisted of $273 billion for free world defense; $389 billion for Social Security, income security and Medicare; $136 billion for net interest expense and $192 billion for all other programs. Spending growth in recent years has been primarily in the areas of free world defense and net interest. Between 1978 and 1986, defense spending has increased by 1.8% of GNP (from 4.8% of total GNP to 6.6%) and net interest expense has increased by 1.7% of GNP. At the same time, the share of GNP spent on general non-defense programs declined by 1.8%. While the deficit is sometimes blamed on a spendthrift America, this weighting towards unpleasant duties at the expense of politically popular social programs directly disproves that claim.

Taxes and expenditures must be equalized in the long run. But if the expenditures are improper—that is, if the expenditures are totally unproductive or not correctly an obligation of the United States government—then raising taxes to pay for them is not justified. Today, major tax increases should be resisted while substantial expenditure eliminations should be made in the two spending areas that have so recently ballooned: the defense budget and the net interest account.

Look first at defense. While there is a legitimate debate as to the necessary amount of free world military expenditure, there can be no debate that the United States pays too much of it.

At the Williamsburg summit of 1983, the heads of all the advanced industrial democracies declared that "the security of our countries is indivisible and must be approached on a global basis." Yet the relative military spending of the democracies does not reflect this shared responsibility. In 1986, the United States spent over 6.5% of its GNP on the free world's common defense while, on average, our allies spent under 3.0%. NATO's European nations collectively spent 3.8% and Japan, the most egregious offender, spent only 1.0%.

The uneven spending among nations is a type of market breakdown well known to Adam Smith: the classic problem of the "free rider." Europe and Japan have been fully protected by the United States even though they have not borne their fair burden. Therefore, they have had no reason to pay more.

The budgetary impact of this free ride is massive. If Europe and Japan would together spend only 4.0% of their GNP on the common good, then the U.S. could reduce its defense burden to approximately 5% of GNP. Although America's defense share would still be disproportionately high, this reduction would save the U.S. roughly $60 billion annually, or almost half of the record 1986 aggregate government deficit.

The alliance's current spending pattern is not justified by our allies' economic hardship. The Second World War is four decades in the past, and Europe and Japan are now America's creditors, not its wards. In the aggregate, the free European economy approximates the economy of the United States and far exceeds the resources of the Soviet Union. Japan, as the world's second leading economic nation, is similarly equipped to play a world role.

Strategically, the long term welfare of the alliance demands that the misallocation be remedied. The U.S. budget and trade deficits, created in part by the present inequity, threaten to turn an angry America toward self-destructive protectionism and unilateral military cutbacks. Either action would dangerously weaken the alliance. The risk is now especially acute towards Japan where, according to a June 1987 *New York Times* poll, 55% of all Japanese already believe that U.S.-Japan relations have become unfriendly. As Zbigniew Brzezinski has warned, "If economic protectionism and other related issues were to weaken or poison American-Japanese relations, the entire structure of U.S. security policy in the Far East would be at risk."

The proper policy direction is clear. Europe and, more particularly, Japan must carry a greater share of the common defense burden.

Europe should be actively encouraged to assume the role of an independent regional power, as Henry Kissinger and others have urged, thereby depolarizing the existing American-Soviet standoff at its point of greatest stress. Already spending close to 4% of collective

GNP on defense and contributing substantial manpower, this role is less a budgetary change than a change in consciousness.

More forceful attention should be focused on Japan, where the spending disparity is greatest and the trade frictions are hottest. Here, it is time for a new U.S.-Japanese peace treaty, welcoming an adult Japan to the full honors and burdens of a leading world power. Due to Japan's sincere antimilitarism and the concerns of Japan's former adversaries, Japan should not rearm. The United States should continue its existing military role in the Pacific. However, Japan must be led to reimburse America for the costs of the U.S. supplied defense (or alternative equivalent expense) up to at least a European-style 4% of the Japanese GNP. Precedent for such sharing has been set by Japanese reimbursements since 1971 for the U.S. marines at Okinawa and by Tokyo's recent pledge to increase Third World foreign aid. Future cost allocation should be based on an explicit mutual understanding that the security interests of Japan and America are now irrevocably intertwined.

In return for Japan's efforts, the United States should pledge to maintain its own dignity and stature as the leading free world nation. This means an end to further "Japan bashing" special interest trade legislation, an end to mercantile currency manipulation and a reaffirmation of America's historical commitments to open markets and to strong allied defense. Such a reallocation and pledge is not the surrender of America's post World War II preeminence. It is the path to its preservation.

Can this new peace be negotiated? That question moves us from Lord Home's incomprehensible back to his merely insoluable. There are, however, reasons to be hopeful. First, because as the effects of the existing spending inequity grows, something will be done. Second, because this is the right thing to do. Trade wars, international animosity and defense breakdowns hurt both America and Japan. In contrast, the sharing of respect and burdens, as proposed here, is consistent with American values and Japanese pride. In the meantime, like the only taxpayer in a two citizen town, America has certain options. While we won't terminate our own services, our displeasure toward our laggard neighbor can take so many forms—diplomatic, cultural, economic—that ultimately, with determined leadership, matters are likely to be resolved.

The second area of improper federal expenditure is America's high interest burden; specifically the high rate of interest that America pays on its $2.4 trillion national debt.

At the time of this writing, the interest rate on a ten year U.S. government bond is over 9%. In contrast, the interest rate on a similarly creditworthy Japanese government bond is under 4%. The interest rate for American long bonds throughout our history, and for the twenty years following World War II, averaged under 5%.

The source of today's excessively high interest cost is monetary instability. The United States government, as owner of the printing press, cannot default on its dollar denominated debts. However, through inflation and currency depreciation, it can and does change the real value of the dollars with which it repays its debts. In today's global capital markets, the world's bond buyers can freely choose among nations and currencies. The risk that they will be repaid in depreciated dollars—that is, in dollars worth less relative to other currencies or to real goods—causes those buyers to demand a high interest rate on dollar denominated debts. If the high rates were caused by other factors, such as the low U.S. savings rate, then financially sophisticated Americans could simply borrow low cost foreign currency and convert their borrowings to dollars. However, most Americans are dissuaded from this course by their own fears that the dollar's value will fall, greatly increasing the nominal expense of foreign currency repayment.

This extra American interest cost—this "instability penalty"—puts a tremendous burden on the federal budget. According to January 1987 estimates of the non-partisan Congressional Budget Office, each one-percentage-point rise in interest rates adds $96 billion of cost to the federal budget over the next five years, starting with an $11 billion cost in 1988 and increasing to over $25 billion per year in 1992. A 4% reduction in interest rates, therefore, back towards the level of Japan and our own stable money past, could save America approximately $400 billion of budget expenses over the next five years and over $100 billion per year by 1992. When added to the roughly $60 billion of defense spending adjustments previously outlined, this savings would have more than eliminated even the largest past aggregate government deficit.

Achieving stable money is entirely a political decision. Its only cost is the forebearance of a "sovereignty" which does not exist and of policy options which do not work.

America and its allies had relatively stable money for two decades following the Second World War as a result of the 1944 Bretton Woods accord. Under this arrangement, America pledged to hold the dollar's value constant against gold while the other nations fixed their currency values to the dollar. This system, however, depended on American economic self-discipline to hold the dollar's value steady and began to disintegrate in the late 1960s. Then, under President Johnson, America too rapidly expanded the money supply in an attempt to simultaneously fund the Great Society welfare programs and the Viet Nam war without a tax increase. As the dollar supply rose rapidly, the real value of each dollar fell, creating inflation throughout the entire interlocked world trading system. In 1971, with our allies balking at this inflation and demanding gold for their cheapened dollars, Bretton Woods came to an end.

After Bretton Woods, currency exchange rates were allowed to float against each other. It was expected that rates would move gently, adjusting gradually according to relative national inflation rates. Instead, the speculative international capital markets have continuously and unpredictably driven exchange rates far above or far below the theoretically proper "purchasing power parity" level; that is, the level where a sum of money can buy the same amount of goods before and after it is exchanged. The devaluation of the dollar in 1971 also reduced the real revenues of the OPEC oil nations and other foreign sellers who priced their goods in dollars, inciting them to raise prices. (In fact, the cost of oil stayed relatively constant in real gold terms all throughout the 1970s even as it skyrocketed in nominal dollar terms.) A good argument can be made that the decade of oil price shocks and world stagflation following 1971 was a direct result of the monetary system's breakdown; another victim of Viet Nam.

Now it is time for a new Bretton Woods. As a first step, the Group of Seven nations—or, at minimum, the U.S., Germany and Japan—should convene an international forum where delegated economists, with the rank of trade ambassador, could develop a shared, technically workable blueprint for currency stabilization. That plan would serve as a focus for public attention and would be returned to the respective polities for debate, discussion and—it is to be hoped—adoption. While the final outlines of such a program are still to be determined, a great deal of academic thought has been devoted to this issue. It is likely that any new arrangement would principally seek to expand the world money supply at a steady and predictable growth rate; that is, it would likely employ Milton Friedman's domestic-focused, anti-inflationary "monetarism" on a more relevant international scale. (See, for example, Ronald I. McKinnon, "An International Standard for Monetary Stabilization", Institute for

International Economics, March 1984). Nations would maintain separate currencies and separate central banks, but would effectively unify their currencies by observing a shared set of monetary growth rules. Self-serving violation of such rules would be seen as an unfair trade practice, subject to the same policing response as adversarial dumping or tariffs.

The Reagan administration's past stabilization efforts, culminating in the February 1987 Louvre arrangement, have been steps in the right direction and should be accelerated. The focus of such efforts must be policy coordination, however, and not merely costly interventions into the speculative currency trading markets. The Federal Reserve can further approximate and facilitate a monetary stabilization agreement by primarily pursuing a "price rule" policy, tightening the money supply as prices begin to rise and easing as prices deflate. In the past, Federal Reserve Board policies have instead focused chiefly on the quantity of money; a measure which has proven increasingly erratic and meaningless as a policy guide. The wholesale price index may be the best focus for such a price rule although, as Federal Reserve Governor Angell and others have argued, commodity prices set daily in world auction markets can be a useful bellweather. Once the dollar's value is anchored against real goods in this way, other nations can voluntarily peg their currency values against the dollar, effectively reinstituting the Bretton Woods principles without a formal accord.

The very notion of an international currency arrangement is sometimes criticized as a politically untenable sacrifice of national sovereignty. In fact, the exact opposite is true. At least since Japan removed its exchange controls in 1980, we and our allies live in a global capital market. Finance is executed worldwide, in a never ending circle of time zones from New York to Tokyo to London. An average $1.5 trillion per day flows through New York's interbank system for foreign and domestic payments; an amount which exceeds the U.S. GNP in three days and the world GNP in three weeks. Like a firehose, this global financial market whips about wildly, "overshooting" and "undershooting" fair exchange rates as the capital flows through it. No single nation has sovereignty over its part of the market if the other nations are moving their parts in chaotically different directions. Either the governments coordinate and all have sovereignty, or no one does.

As with American states sharing a common U.S. dollar, nations in a stabilized currency block would be free to compete on some fronts but not on others. Interest rates, inflation rates and monetary growth would be the same across national borders. Investment, education, taxes, wages, etc. would differ.

In short, nations in a world of sound money would have to play their economics straight. First, governments would have to fund themselves openly—through taxes or borrowing—rather than through the inflationary printing of new money. As America's Viet Nam experience proved, the printing press alternative is ultimately futile and often an attempt to evade political as well as monetary discipline. Second, nations would have to discard the Phillips Curve approach to full employment; the now discredited theory that creating inflation is necessary to create jobs. The decline of both inflation and unemployment in recent years demonstrates that the Phillips Curve's allegedly inexorable jobs: inflation trade-off does not exist. Instead monetary disorder, by weakening nations, costs jobs. Third, nations would have to let market pressures improve or penalize the performance of their inefficient citizens. Governments would have to abandon the attempt to evade honest competition through continual currency devaluations.

A constantly falling dollar is at times said to be justified, or is even encouraged, as the "solution" to America's trade deficit. It is true that a falling dollar makes America poorer relative to other nations, and that poor, low wage nations can buy less and sell more than rich nations. Still, by definition, self-inflicted poverty cannot be the path to national prosperity. Nor is it fair to destroy the wealth of the nation's savers and efficient citizens in order to shield overcompensated and inefficient citizens from honest foreign competitors. Additionally, even if a mercantile devaluation strategy were desirable, it is not easy to implement. Many of America's toughest trading partners, such as Korea and Taiwan, peg their currency to the dollar. As our currency drops in value, so do their currencies, and no trade ground is gained. Even if Americans buy fewer units of foreign goods, the devaluation causes the nominal dollar costs of those units to rise, eliminating the statistical trade benefit sought. (This is the down slope of the economists' so called "J curve," a temporary phenomenon in theory which has proven to be disturbingly perpetual in practice.) Finally, the American workers and companies which were internationally competitive before the devaluation will refuse to have undeserved poverty thrust upon them, and will ultimately raise their wages and prices back to the real international value levels which their services can command. These domestic price increases, plus the increased nominal dollar cost of foreign imports, are likely to spark inflation and leave America even worse off than before. A slow runner cannot become fast by changing the length of a mile in his own mind. And just as we do not change the length of an inch or the weight of a pound with each month's trade figures, the buying power of the dollar and other currencies should be set at real purchasing power parities and maintained there.

Our budget deficit is a long term structural problem. The remedies proposed—reallocation of allied defense costs and monetary stabilization—are long term, structural solutions. The time is ripe for both approaches, but in the near term, the government should maintain its current course and seek to contain the deficit problem by slow growth in expenditures. As Senator Phil Gramm has argued, even a moderate level of economic growth can generate about $70 billion of additional federal revenues each year without tax increases. This is more than enough revenue to meet the original Gramm-Rudman-Hollings deficit reduction targets if spending is held constant. In controlling costs, particular attention should be focused on the cure of existing administrative inefficiencies, on entitlement programs which are paid without regard to the recipient's need and on cost of living adjustments which increase more rapidly than national per capita wage growth.

Low National Savings

The resolution of the budget deficit as outlined would resolve a number of related problems: first, America's low national savings rate.

In 1987, America's gross savings was only 12.6% of GNP ($566 billion) compared with 13.8% of GNP ($551 billion) in 1985 and 16.3% of GNP ($445 billion) in 1980. The principal cause of this decline is the federal budget deficit which, by definition, is a "dissaving" and a direct reduction to the total national savings figure. Eliminating the $153 billion aggregate government budget deficit in 1987 would have raised the national savings rate back to the original private, state and local savings level of $719 billion. That level is a healthy 16.0% of GNP and was sufficient to fund the strong 1987 private investment demand of $716 billion.

Despite alarmist claims to the contrary, the recent savings performance of the private sector has been consistent with the nation's historical experience. Private savings is made up of business savings and household savings. Business savings is by far the larger portion, accounting for over 80% of the total. Such business savings has been growing every year since 1958, and was 12.3% of GNP ($553 billion) in 1986 compared to 12.5% ($341 billion) in 1980 and 10.5% ($107 billion) in 1970.

The smaller and much scrutinized household savings component declined to $120 billion in 1987, from $130 billion in 1986 and a peak of $164 billion in 1984. The apparent problem is primarily due, however, to the quirks of statistical measurement. First, the technical definition of savings does not include increases in household wealth from capital gains. Second, the savings figure is reduced by short-term credit card debt, much of which is accrued as a convenient substitute for cash rather than as a result of financial need. Third, the overall debt picture is skewed by demographic factors. The postwar baby boom generation has moved into the twenty-five to forty-four year age category, the period when individuals commonly set up their households and raise children. In life's normal course, the inherently high debt demands of this period are repaid with the higher income achieved in the working years after age forty-four.

The best measure of a household's wealth and creditworthiness is its total net worth; that is, the surplus of all its assets (including stocks, bonds and the family home) over all its debts. On a national basis, such household net worth has grown steadily, reaching a total of $13.5 trillion in late 1987 compared to $10.4 trillion in 1986 and $8.0 trillion in 1980. The October 1987 stock market crash reduced this net worth by an estimated $1 trillion, but the loss was offset by the equally dramatic bull market gains in 1987's first nine months. Importantly, the household net worth is also highly liquid. Household financial assets approximately equaled total debts, including such long term debt as home mortgages, and was a strong 2.5 times total debts when home mortgages are excluded. The American consumer has not been profligate, and America's annual private savings performance is consistent with traditional levels when this rich build-up of assets is considered.

America's International Debt

America's newfound position as the world's largest international debtor is a second direct result of the budget deficit.

America's foreign debts now exceed $200 billion and are commonly forecasted to exceed $500 billion by 1990. The cost of servicing such debts will be a growing burden on the domestic economy, and the possible sudden withdrawal of foreign credit poses a continuing national risk.

Foreign debt has been a necessary evil, however, to finance critically important private sector investment at a time when the government deficit has used up so much domestic capital. The alternatives to such foreign debt are even worse, requiring the "crowding out" of productive private investment or an inflationary surge in the money supply. As economist Herbert Stein has explained: "In 1986 . . . U.S. individuals and corporations saved $680 billion gross and government (federal, state and local) borrowed $143 billion to finance its deficits. If there had been no capital inflow, private investment in the U.S. could not have exceeded $537 billion. Since there was a capital inflow of $144 billion, however, private investment of $686 billion was possible and occurred." Arguably, the earnings from the additional private investment made possible by the foreign debt will be sufficient to repay that debt, and the inflow is a social positive.

Once the government deficit is eliminated, existing national savings will be sufficient to fund existing national investment needs. The net demand for foreign capital inflows would end. In sum, the real culprit is the budget deficit, not the loans. The real anomaly is that America must borrow money from its allies at high interest, which it then returns to those allies at no charge for their defense needs.

The Trade Deficit

The nation's $153 billion trade deficit is a third direct result of the budget deficit and the mirror image of the capital inflow problem. Just as debits must equal credits on a bookkeeper's ledger, the necessary offset to the capital surplus is a current account deficit and their genesis is the same. As Stanford economist Ronald I. McKinnon has explained, "The fiscal deficit creates a shortage of savings in this economy and then we borrow from foreigners to cover that shortfall, and that creates the trade deficit. That group of facts remains no matter how you set the exchange rate." Or as the 1987 Economic Report of the President has more formally stated, "This unprecedented deterioration of the U.S. fiscal position during an expansion, combined with a normal cyclical decline in the private saving-investment balance, has been reflected in an unprecedented deterioration in the U.S. current account balance."

In frustration or economic self-interest, the trade deficit is often attributed to other causes, including unfair trade, low foreign wages, slow foreign growth and the decline of American manufacturing. However, the facts do not support these explanations.

Look first to the role of unfair trade. The United States ran a balanced trade position until our budget problems began, including an $11.6 billion trading surplus against non-OPEC countries in 1981. As trade economists Robert Z. Lawrence and Robert E. Litan have written, " . . . To account for the turnaround of the overall U.S. trade deficit, unfair foreign practices must suddenly and uniformly have led to change around 1981. Indeed, there must have been something close to a massive global conspiracy. Yet we know that protection is not much greater in the rest of the world today than in 1981; the Europeans have cut back on their industrial subsidies and the Japanese market is now somewhat more open. Actually, protection has probably risen more in the United States than in any other market."

Japan is often accused of the greatest improprieties, but while our trade deficit with Japan has been growing, it has only been growing in line with the trade deficit generally. Between 1982 and 1986, the U.S. bilateral trade positioned worsened against all of the top 10 U.S. trading partners, not just Japan, and against 19 of the top 20. Nor is the Japanese market closed to U.S. brand goods. From Big Macs to IBM computers, the Japanese consume over twice as many U.S. goods per capita as Americans consume of Japanese goods. However, a majority of those American goods are manufactured by U.S. corporations at facilities off U.S. soil and therefore are not counted as exports in the U.S. trade figures. In contrast, Japan's less mature multinationals have only recently begun to set up manufacturing operations abroad.

Similarly, the deficit is not due to systematic trade losses to low wage countries. Such countries now account for less of our imports than they did in 1960 (when Japan was in that category). Superior capital investment and productivity offset low wages. To again quote Lawrence and Litan, "If developing countries had our skills, technology and capital levels, their wages wouldn't be so low." Average wages in Japan are approaching the U.S. level and the average wages in trade-surplus rich West Germany exceed ours.

Nor is the trade deficit due to slow growth abroad, although this, like unfair trade, contributes to the problem. Chronic deflation in the West German and Japanese currencies indicates that these economies should be stimulated, as the Reagan administration has urged. However, only a fraction of any such growth is likely to be spent on imports, and only a fraction of that on U.S. imports. According to Martin Feldstein, former chairman of President Reagan's Council of Economic Advisers, "Even doubling the projected real growth rates in the rest of the industrial world for this year (1987) and next would cut the 1988 trade deficit by less than $20 billion."

Finally, the trade deficit is not due to chronic mismanagement or the decline of America's manufacturing base. In 1960, at the peak of America's economic preeminence, manufacturing output was $144 billion, or slightly over 21% of the nation's real non-farm gross domestic product. In 1986, after years of an overvalued dollar and intense foreign competition, manufacturing output was $824 billion, or slightly over 22% of gross domestic product. In 1986, even as the trade deficit grew, America's 3.5% increase in manufacturing labor productivity led the industrialized world. Since the business cycle peak in 1981, America's manufacturing productivity has grown at a 3.8% annual rate, almost 50% faster than the nation's post-war average rate and more than twice the rate between 1973 and 1981. America needs government policy, not industrial policy.

Unavoidably, the trade deficit analysis must return to the budget deficit and America's aggregate spending-saving imbalance. When a nation (including its government) demands more goods than that nation produces, it will inevitably turn to foreign suppliers to make up the difference. It will run a trade deficit.

National demand has three components: investment, consumption and government spending. Therefore, at any given level of GNP, there are three fundamental ways to reduce the trade gap: (1) reduce private investment; (2) reduce private consumption (i.e., raise private savings); or (3) reduce government spending.

The first demand component, investment, is critical to national economic growth. If the trade deficit is simply the application of foreign savings to private American investment (or to government "investment" in national infrastructure), then the trade deficit is beneficial and should actually be encouraged. The United States ran exactly this type of beneficent growth deficit during its rapid expansion in the nineteenth century. Japan ran such a deficit from the end of World War II until the 1980s.

Unfortunately, too much investment is not the source of our current trade deficit. Domestic savings could satisfy domestic investment if there was no government deficit, and government spending on long term capital projects has not drastically increased.

Nor is private consumption too high or savings too low. Savings are in line with prudence given the high level of household net worth, and it would be unfair and recessionary to tax the private sector to pay for military and interest expenditures that our government should not be making in the first place. Government spending is the key. And given this cause and effect, the proper policy directions for the trade problem are apparent.

First, the government budget deficit must be cut.

Second, and just as importantly, the budget deficit must be cut in the right way; through stable money and increased allied defense spending. Simply balancing the books by a tax increase, at the expense of private investment and growth, would be a worse result than the trade deficit itself. In contrast, increased military spending by Japan and West Germany would not only cut our deficit but could be structured to stimulate those economies as currently desired. Stable currencies would not only reduce interest costs but would prevent a reoccurrence of the dollar overvaluation which crippled American competitiveness in 1981 through 1985.

Third, protectionism must be resisted. Unfair trade practices are not the principal cause of our trade imbalance and should not be used as a defense for self-interested corporate and labor lobbying. A trade war strategy will only lead to retaliation, slower growth world-wide and a weaker alliance. Protective tariffs are ultimately a secret tax on the innocent, subsidizing the nations inefficient at the expense of closed foreign markets for efficient American businesses and higher prices for American consumers. According to economists Gary Hufbauer and Howard Rosen, existing protectionist measures cost American consumers $53 billion in 1984 alone. Programs which highlight these costs should be supported, such as Jack Kemp and Phil Gramm's proposed "consumer impact statements" for trade legislation. The president, pursuing broader goals, should continue to hold the power to overrule specific industry protections recommended by the International Trade Commission.

Fourth, if trade protection is granted, such protection should be made for a limited term only and made in the form of tariffs, not quotas. Over time, existing quotas should be converted to their tariff equivalent by auction, with rights to U.S. market access sold to the highest bidder. Unlike traditional quotas, tariffs and auctioned quotas provide revenue for the federal government—a potential $7 billion in 1986—which is now left as undeserved profit for foreign sellers. Additionally, tariffs and auctioned quotas permit efficient importers to gain market share while traditional quotas merely preserve the status quo. As explicit barriers, tariffs can be explicitly removed when free trade is restored.

Finally, while not the root of our problem, foreign unfair trade practices do exist and must be fought more efficiently. The administration's current agenda for the Uruguay round of international trade talks should be supported and accelerated, including more effective dispute resolution, fair trade in services and in agriculture and respect for intellectual property rights.

Third World Debt

The Third World debt problem is really two separate issues: first, the perpetual poverty of the developing world's nations and second, the tenuous solvency of the commercial banks which have lent to them.

The world's poor countries now carry over $1 trillion of total debt, to be serviced against per capita incomes as low as Ethiopia's $110 per year. Latin American debt totals almost $400 billion, including $109 billion owed by Brazil, $107 billion owed by Mexico, $52 billion by Argentina and $35 billion by Venezeula. Mexico defaulted on its debt in August 1982, and the banks rescheduled payments. In February 1987, Brazil withheld interest on its $68 billion bank debt, including $24 billion owed to American banks. Ecuador stopped paying on its debts in March 1987 and today, Bolivia, Costa Rica, Cuba, Honduras, Nicaragua and Peru are also in the "can't pay" or "won't pay" categories, while Argentina is wavering.

These defaults and potential defaults put the creditor banks at great risk. In Fall 1987, Citibank's $14.8 billion portfolio of less developed country ("LDC") loans was almost twice as large as its $7.8 billion net worth. Bank of America had $9.5 billion of LDC loans against a $3.4 billion net worth. Manufacturers Hanover has $9.0 billion of loans against a $3.2 billion net worth. In May 1987, Citibank reserved for $3.0 billion of potential loan write-offs, reducing the carrying amount of its LDC debt to approximately 75% of face value. Other major banks soon followed. Unfortunately, the foreign debt is worth only about 60% of face value in the open market, indicating that further major writedowns may still be necessary.

Both the banks and the debtor nations would be greatly aided by the monetary reform policies already recommended in this essay. In the 1970s, worldwide inflation and the resulting petrodollar deposits emboldened the banks to make their Third World loans. In the 1980s,

worldwide deflation, falling commodity prices and rising dollar interest rates triggered the present crisis. Steady aggregate price levels
and lower long term interest rates—outgrowths of stable currency—
would benefit both lenders and borrowers.

The key to survival for the commercial banks is time to outgrow
their problems. In this context, the banks' continuing "rollovers" and
rescheduling of the uncollectible debt is sound practice. Each year,
the banks are able to reduce their relative LDC debt exposure by
expanding their other assets and by selling or writing down parts of
their LDC loan portfolio. This diversification effort would be enhanced by the continued development of a private financial market
for LDC world debt where banks could sell their loans (at an appropriate discount) to speculative buyers. Such a market now exists but
totalled only about $2.5 billion in 1986. Its growth is being actively
undertaken by fee conscious investment banks and could be further
sped by permitting banks to amortize losses on loan sales over a
number of years.

The banks and debtor nations would also benefit from increased
use of debt-equity swaps, whereby the creditors exchange their debt
for interest-free, equity investments in the debtor's economy. Approximately $5 billion of such swaps were performed in 1986. The
chief obstacle to more swaps now is the lack of desirable investment
opportunities. One solution is for the debtor nations to offer the
banks the local currency at a discount (for example, $12 million worth
of peso investments to repay a $10 million face value loan). Alter-
nately, debt repayments could be accumulated in bank controlled,
local currency-denominated investment funds and spent over time.

As these debt-equity swap proposals recognize, the debtor nations
also need time and money to overcome their problems. Economies
such as Brazil's have the capacity to achieve real prosperity, but are
crippled by the need to apply the bulk of their export revenues to
annual debt service. The Reagan administration's original "Baker
Plan" properly emphasized Third World growth by encouraging the
extension of new bank loans. Such new loans, however, should be
given credit seniority over old loans, just as fresh loans to a company
in bankruptcy are given seniority over the loans which put it there.
Otherwise—with existing LDC loans trading at only 60% of face
value—banks would effectively lose 40% of any new loans they
extend; an immediate loss of $8 billion on the $20 billion of new bank
lines sought by the original Baker Plan.

Finally, the respective roles of the banks and their governments must be properly defined. In truth, capital infusions to Third World nations are less business transactions than foreign aid. Unlike domestic lending, the banks never had proper financial reports on the LDC borrowers; never knew how much the nations were borrowing from other sources; could not control the use of the borrowed funds and cannot now enforce collection. At the same time, the banks' profit—motivated actions bear heavily on free world security, threatening to topple numerous friendly foreign governments. Future Third World sovereign loans might best be channelled through the U. S. government or an international development agency such as the World Bank. The commercial banks would make risk free loans to this agency at an appropriately low interest rate. The agency, in turn, would loan those funds to the developing nations—perhaps at an equally low interest rate—and control collection.

Jobs

Jobs and job creation comprise both America's great success story and a problem of the first magnitude. The overall employment trend is promising while sectoral problems of great difficulty remain.

In Spring 1988, the unemployment rate was approximately 5.5%, the lowest level since the Republican year of 1974. In total, since 1970, the U.S. has created more than thirty million new jobs and total employment has increased 40%. More than fourteen million new jobs have been created since the 1982 recession. In contrast, West Germany and the U.K. have unemployment rates of 8.9% and 8.8%, respectively, and had negligible job growth since 1970. Even the fabled Japanese economy has increased employment by only 15% since 1970. The Japanese unemployment rate is commonly reported at around 3%, but is calculated on a different statistical measure. Laid-off workers with benefits and those working under fifteen hours a week are classified among the employed in Japan, but classified as unemployed in the U.S. Applying U.S. measures, the Japanese unemployment rate is closer to 5.0%.

The quality of the new American jobs is a subject of intense debate but appears to be generally satisfactory. A widely quoted study by Barry Bluestone and Bennett Harrison has argued that 58% of the new jobs have been in the low-wage category. However, the Bluestone-Harrison study focused only on the 1979 to 1984 time frame, which included two years of the disastrous Carter administration, the Fed's fight against inflation and the deep 1981–1982 recession. Looking just at the Reagan years of 1981 to 1985, only 6% of the new jobs have been in low-wage categories, while the middle and high-pay categories split the remaining new jobs evenly.

Concern is also expressed about part-time employment, which is growing faster than full-time employment. This is a world phenomenon, however, and since 1973 the relative rate of U.S. full-time—part-time growth has been better than in any industrialized nation except Ireland and Italy. Overall, in 1985, U.S. part-time employment was 17% of full-time employment, compared to 17% in Japan, 12% in West Germany, 16% in Canada and 21% in Britain.

The longer term outlook for jobs is excellent. Now that the baby boom generation has entered the work force, there will be a decline in new U.S. workers even as available jobs continue to increase. This should lead to a tightening labor market and better job opportunity. The recent Labor Department study, *Workforce 2000*, predicts a 10% increase in jobs by 1995 joined to a 10% reduction in the number of 16 to 24 year olds entering the labor force.

Serious challenges remain along with this good news, however. First, the unemployed must be given the skills to fill these available jobs. Future jobs will require increasing education. The *Workforce 2000* study estimates that high school graduation or better will be needed for 86% of the jobs created between now and the year 2000 and college graduation or better will be needed for 30% of future jobs. In contrast, today, the high school dropout rate is 18% for blacks and 29% for Hispanics. As many as 30 million adult Americans are functionally illiterate, including—according to a 1982 Labor Department study—an estimated 50%–70% of the unemployed. A strengthened educational system is imperative and a cornerstone of progressive Republican policy.

America's second employment challenge is the decline in traditional manufacturing employment. The manufacturing sector and manufacturing jobs have become "decoupled"; that is, because of automation and operating efficiencies, the manufacturing sector is prospering even as its labor force shrinks. In 1960, manufacturing accounted for 21% of the U.S. non-agricultural gross domestic product and 31% of all non-agricultural jobs. In 1986, manufacturing accounted for 22% of U.S. gross domestic product, but only 19% of employment. Even this severely reduced employment level may still be too high if America is to remain internationally competitive. In Japan, for example, 670,000 workers (including employees of subcontractors and outside parts manufacturers) build eleven million cars a year. In Detroit, two million workers build ten million cars; approximately three times as many workers per car. Two million net manufacturing jobs have been lost since 1979 and the loss of more jobs is likely. The workers losing these high-wage manufacturing jobs are rarely the workers winning the new high-wage service sector jobs.

The government's most important role in this issue is to keep the economy growing, maximizing alternative opportunities. To this end, recessionary tax increases should be avoided. Interest rates should be lowered. Antitrust rules should be loosened for troubled industries. Also more adult education and worker retraining programs should be adopted, as former Labor Secretary Bill Brock's call for a $980 million jobs program recognized. The principal solutions to this problem, however, will be drafted on the shop floor. The United Auto Workers made job security the central issue of their recent labor negotiations. The Communications Workers and the United Steelworkers have done the same, trading wages and work rule demands for retraining programs, income insurance and "no layoff" policies. IBM, among other non-unionized companies, has adopted these approaches voluntarily, as a central management ethic. In a global marketplace, the transition to lower employment levels in mature industries cannot be stopped. A blanket opposition to manufacturing efficiencies will only lead to the fall of entire industries to foreign competitors. The goal, instead, must be to develop new industries and to share the cost of transition equitably between workers and shareholders.

POVERTY

A rising tide does not lift sunken boats, and a strong economy cannot be relied upon as the sole cure for poverty. Structural poverty is chiefly a social problem, not an economic one. As Britain's *Economist* has observed, "An American's chance of staying poor is less than ½% if he or she does the following three things: (a) completes high school; (b) gets and stays married; and (c) stays employed, even if initially only at the minimum wage. Americans who fail these three requirements have an up-to-80 times greater chance of staying for a long time below the official poverty line, and breeding sad generations there."

Poverty must first be fought through educational policy. More emphasis should be placed on preschool and elementary education, particularly on reading skills as the key to self-help. The Head Start concept should be revived, parent involvement expanded and funding provided to reduce teacher: student ratios in the early years. Secondary education would benefit from increased interaction with colleges and with the private sector; programs such as job and scholarship guarantees for students meeting set achievement criteria. Motivation is based on the size of a reward times the probability of achieving that reward. Disadvantaged students must be convinced of the value of education and given confidence that the rewards are within their reach.

Second, poverty must be fought through policies which strengthen the family. As Senator Moynihan and others have argued, welfare should be reformed to extend eligibility to needy two-parent families. Teenage mothers should be required to remain with other family members and to finish school. Stronger action should be taken to determine paternity and to enforce payment of child support.

Third, the fight against poverty must be brought back to a human level. The poverty problem is too frequently shunted off to a professional welfare bureaucracy and forgotten. Broadbased volunteer programs, such as the "Big Brothers/Big Sisters" effort and Senator Kennedy's proposed "Literacy Corps," can supplement these efforts with a needed level of personalized support. The promotion and funding of such volunteer programs should be increased, and a public service requirement considered as a prerequisite for graduation from federally funded colleges. Tax deductions should be considered for contributions of time to charitable projects, as well as for contributions of money.

Finally, the mix of existing poverty and minority advancement programs can be shifted to apply existing expenditures more effectively. A prime example of misuse is the Federal Communication Commission's minority certificate program, which permits a seller of a television station to perpetually defer capital gains tax if the buyer is black, Hispanic or Native American. As the *Washington Post* has reported, under this rule, one white-owned media conglomerate, Gaylord Broadcasting, recently avoided paying well over $100 million of tax by selling its Florida television station to a second white-owned media conglomerate, Gillett Broadcasting, which had teamed up with a black lawyer. The lawyer invested no money in the deal and has an option to be bought out by Gillett for $1 million after two years. In short, the U.S. government sacrificed $100 million of revenue to give one already successful lawyer $1 million. In contrast, total federal outlays for adult education in 1986 were only $104 million. Needless

Gaylord sale is only one example of the minority certificate program and the minority certificate program is only one example of misspent funds. (New York, for example, pays $1,600 per month per room to house the homeless in less than palatial welfare hotels.) Such misuses should be systematically eradicated, with the savings specifically earmarked for the expansion of more useful poverty programs.

ECONOMIC POLITICS

Economic policy is the key to domestic political success for the progressive Republican movement and for its rivals. President Reagan's alleged 1984 conservative mandate was really an economic mandate. Voters who said their own political views matched Mondale's, but that they would be better off financially under Reagan, were for the president by greater than 80 to 20. Voters who thought that Mondale would be better than Reagan at reducing the threat of nuclear war, but that they personally would be better off under Reagan, supported the president 68 to 31. Those who thought that Mondale would better ensure that government programs are fair to all, but that they personally would be better off under Reagan, supported Reagan by 71 to 27.

The free market oriented directions outlined in this essay are consistent with the electorate's concern for economic prosperity and with the broader progressive political philosophy. It is not coincidence that Adam Smith's *Wealth of Nations* and the Declaration of Independence were penned in the same year. Both, and ultimately our Constitution, reflect the fundamental tenets of John Locke's political Age of Enlightenment which still guide and define progressives: a reliance on rationality, a belief in the possibility of social progress through social organization, an emphasis on individuals first and the government as the instrument of their collective will.

The progressive economic approach differs substantially from the competing economic approaches of the traditional Democrats, neoliberal Democrats, traditional Republicans and supply-side Republicans. The traditional, organized labor, Democrats pursue desirable ends with counterproductive means. Their goals of full employment, an end to poverty and higher wages are extremely important ones and are shared by progressive Republicans. However, their non-market or anti-market policies are frequently overly simple and ignore second order effects. If wages are low, they say, raise them. If imports are gaining market share, prohibit them. If people are poor, force the wealthier to give them money. Unfortunately, each mandated positive action can be accompanied by an even greater negative market reaction—a cut in jobs, a trade war, a taxpayer revolt, inflation, lower productivity, recession. These market forces can be ignored by monopolies, and in the days of "closed system" economics and undisputed American economic supremacy, such monopolies existed. Unions had a monopoly over the labor supply in many industries and the U.S. government had a monopoly over national macroeconomic conditions. In our brave new international system, however, these monopolies no longer exist. Traditional Democratic policies, which still implicitly rely on such anti-market power, inevitably break down and leave the U.S. only uncompetitive and frustrated.

The new model "neoliberal" Democrats acknowledge the shortcomings of their ideological forebears but replace them with flaws of their own. Like the Swiss dadaist who wrote his name in the snow and called it "The Alps," younger Democratic politicians have discovered the existence of private enterprise and called it "neoliberalism". As such, their ideas are noteworthy primarily to the extent that they correct the Democrats' own past mistakes, while so delayed a comprehension leads to fears of future backsliding and confusion.

The market system competes for neoliberal affections against two distinctly anti-market schools of thought: the social interventionist model of the Great Society, and E. F. Schumacher's "Small is Beautiful" approach of the Aquarian late '60s and early '70s. The result is a strange, often self-contradictory set of policies. Neoliberals support business, but only small business; the type of clean Silicon Valley operation that fits easily with the ideals of Woodstock, but which has only limited application in the real world. As "Atari Democrats" in 1984, the neoliberals pledged to lead the national transition into the new "sunrise" world of small semiconductor firms. Not surprisingly, the subsequent performance of both Atari videogames and underfunded semiconductor makers was anything but sunny. Neoliberals openly espouse Schumpeterian "creative destruction" and entrepreneurial risk, but propose to mummify our economy with endless tripartite panels of Big Labor, Big Management and Big Government. One must wonder in their call for a new national Family, who will be the children and who the parents.

Finally, the focus of neoliberal policies is alternately too small and too large. Their best proposals—such as an increased use of bonuses and stock ownership to enhance labor wage flexibility—are private management policies, not government policies. Other neoliberal ideas—such as Robert Reich's call for a new American mythology—are beyond the reach of legislation. The real work of government—the macroeconomic work of managing the alliance, lowering interest rates, stabilizing the dollar—is given far too little attention.

Traditional Republicans correctly focus on the macroeconomic aggregates, but in the wrong way. First, their justifiable concern with the budget deficit leads to unjustified calls for higher taxes. The broad based, structural solutions are overlooked. Second, in the past, Republican Keynesians have sought to manipulate the macroeconomic aggregates to control private sector performance. Such efforts at "fine tuning" ultimately proved fruitless and collapsed under the Keynesian theoretical impossibility of stagflation. Progressive economics, in contrast, rejects fine tuning and seeks only to make the aggregates fair and predictable so that private individuals can control their own destiny.

Supply-side economics must be technically faulted on two grounds. First, it has placed too much reliance on marginal tax rate policy without sufficient empirical support and without regard to accompanying economic conditions. The specific impact of tax rate reduction on growth, savings and investment is still largely a matter of conjecture, while the explosion in the federal budget and trade deficits under Reagan casts a dark shadow. Second, the gold standard does not seem the optimal way to seek needed monetary reform. The use of gold is unnecessary and immediately confuses the monetary debate with the visions of robber barons and William Jennings Bryan, "gold bugs" and South Africa. It makes an already difficult political issue impossible. Furthermore, setting the right initial parity price for gold would be extremely difficult; too low a price would lead to world inflation, while too high a price would lead to world deflation. Finally, the world gold supply is almost certain to grow at a different rate than the world economy, necessitating numerous difficult and destabilizing shifts in the gold parity value.

The principal problem with supply-side economics, however, is the ideological company it keeps. The best supply-side thought—such as Robert Mundell's work on international economics and Lew Lehrman's calls for monetary stability—have been critically important and correct. However, through electoral circumstance and coalition politics, these forward thinking economic approaches have become politically entangled with some exceedingly backward social approaches; ideas such as racial segregation at colleges and the mandatory teaching of creationism as science. A free marketplace in goods belongs with a free marketplace of ideas. Economic freedoms belong with personal freedoms. Many of the best supply-side spokesmen, such as George Gilder, began their careers as progressive Republicans. Perhaps, it is time they returned.

CONCLUSION

Here, then, are the core elements of a progressive Republican economic platform:

• A fairer allocation of the common allied defense costs among all the allies, thereby reducing America's budget and trade deficits and America's reliance on foreign borrowings.

• A return to stable exchange rates through the coordination of allied monetary policies, thereby reducing American interest rates and restoring order to the international marketplace. Lower interest rates would further reduce America's budget and trade deficits, aid Third World debtor nations and buoy American competitiveness.

• Continued support of free trade, enhanced by faster response to specific unfair trade practices and other reforms.

• An emphasis on long term policy consistency and reasonableness; a refusal to trigger a real economic recession through symbolic quick tax or spending fixes.

• Continued reductions in unemployment through economic growth, favorable demographic trends and a strengthened educational system.

• A direct attack on severe structural poverty through education and family policy, broad based community efforts and a more effective expenditure mix among existing poverty programs.

• An economic approach that is more free market oriented than Democratic Party proposals, more global in scope than the traditional Republican doctrines and more concerned with social reform than current supply-side views.

Real advances are possible in the economic arena, as in other areas of social concern. Progressive Republicans—by championing their traditional principles of rationality, individual liberty, social justice, internationalism and institutional reform—can contribute meaningfully to that advance.

Making Self-Government Work: Recruiting The Best for Public Service

Ambassador Elliot L. Richardson

Just two hundred years ago the debate in Philadelphia between the advocates of a strong national government and the defenders of small government was winding down. The final bargains had been struck, and the Committee on Style was putting the finishing touches on the resulting compromises. The structure thus erected, with only such later augmentations of national power as practical necessity demanded and judicial interpretation allowed, has held up remarkably well under the increasingly heavy burdens thrust upon it by growth and change. As time passes the magnitude of this achievement looms ever larger.

Happily, many of the issues that divided the framers—slavery and property qualifications for voters, for example—have long since been put to rest. Not so the debate over strong vs. weak government. The Reagan Revolution is only the latest battle in a war that has never known a truce. But this conflict too is winding down. In a book written more than ten years ago, I argued that the federal government was already confronted by excessive demands. The resulting tendency toward top-heaviness, intrusiveness and remoteness from popular understanding and control had to be resisted. Any new program, therefore, should be required to sustain a heavy burden of justification.

All this is even clearer now. Today's challenge is to keep the federal government from being totally overwhelmed by the additional tasks that no other level of government is equipped to perform.

The list of new demands is long and depressing: cleaning up toxic wastes, softening the blow of catastrophic illness, insuring air safety, deterring insider trading, containing terrorism, holding down the escalation of health-care costs, restricting nuclear hazards, combating the AIDs pandemic, promoting competitivenes, fighting drug abuse, overcoming the trade imbalance, shoring up distressed S&Ls, coping with the social strains consequent upon an emerging underclass, helping welfare mothers find work and obtain day care, etc., etc. If this daunting array is to receive any response at all, it can only be in a manner that makes the most efficient possible use of limited political, managerial and fiscal capacity. Today's constraints on federal ambition are practical, not ideological. They will not go out with the conservative tide. That is why no one—not even the most liberal of the Democratic Presidential candidates—has seen fit to come forward with a new version of the Great Society.

Similar necessities drive the decentralization of government in countries where the concentration of power has long been grossly excessive. Stimulated by China's example, most of the world's state central systems are beginning to open up their economies and create room for market forces. Even the USSR is belatedly reacting to the awareness that rigidity, the stifling of initiative and the retardation of economic growth are inevitable consequences of central control. In these countries the process is not simply non-ideological but counter-ideological. It demonstrates once again that there is nothing so powerful as a fact whose time has come.

But we who affirm the values inherent in free self-government have additional and more compelling reasons for resisting any further enlargement of national power. We see the right to have a voice, to be heard and to have some impact on the forces that shape our lives as intrinsic to individual dignity and freedom. We still share with the Constitution-makers the same concern with protecting these ultimate values that led them to limit and separate the powers of government. Although they disagreed as to exactly what powers must as a practical matter be conferred by their states on the new national government, they were of one mind on the point that it should have only those powers that the new Constitution would expressly delegate. As the Tenth Amendment later confirmed, all powers not so delegated were "reserved to the States respectively, or to the people." This great leap beyond Locke and Montesquieu, who took it for granted that there was no limit on the aggregate power whose separation they espoused, inspired and made credible the preamble's "We the People."

So far, who could disagree? No true conservative would quarrel with any of these points; they could go straight into a speech by Ronald Reagan and look right at home. Many conservatives, however, hang back from one of the most important conclusions that follows from this exposition. It is that their nation now needs better motivated, better trained, more experienced, better qualified, and better paid public servants than ever before—and that this requirement will continue to grow as far ahead as we can see.

Why does this follow? Because (1) serious new problems that cry out for government action are continuing to multiply while (2) the government's capacity both to deal with these problems and to handle its existing responsibilities is not keeping pace and (3) the intrusiveness of government into our daily lives has already gone disturbingly far. Responding to (1) while reckoning with (2) and showing proper concern for (3) will take some doing. The risks of failure are risks not only to our well-being and prosperity but to our freedom.

How well we succeed in meeting these challenges will thus depend on the knowledge, skill and ingenuity with which government policies and programs are shaped and administered. They must be so designed and conducted as to entail the least possible restriction of individual freedom while at the same time dealing effectively with the circumstances that compel some degree of intervention. Sophisticated program evaluation, risk assessment, and hardheaded cost-benefit analysis are indispensable tools. There is an equal need, meanwhile, to find ways of cutting back the federal government's existing functions so that essential new tasks can be tackled without increasing its total burden. The options include turning programs over to the states and localities, involving the private sector, simplifying regulations, and phasing out programs that have served their purpose or that have not been effective. Selecting the right mix of these devices is another test of knowledge, skill and ingenuity.

But this trio of qualities is only a beginning. Courage and imagination are also needed. So too are good judgment, the ability to work with others, to motivate them, and to maintain discipline. Experience helps, together with the wisdom it teaches.

These attributes don't come off the shelf. They're in short supply. As the baby boom gets grayer, competition for the best and brightest among the next, numerically smaller, generation will be keener. If government is to attract and hold its needed share of talent, the rewards and satisfactions of government service, which for more than a decade have lagged further and further behind other occupations, will have to be increased.

The problem is already serious. Its disturbing implications were ably set forth last year in a clear, dispassionate, and thoroughly documented paper on "The Federal Service at the Crossroads" by Charles H. Levine and Rosslyn S. Kleeman. Prepared for a conference held in September, 1986 by the Brookings Institution and the American Enterprise Institute for Public Policy Research (AEI), the paper called attention to "a policy stalemate between Congress and the White House" that is leading to "a civil service that many believe is unable to attract, retain, and appropriately deploy people with the skills and motivation needed for the tasks government faces now and in the next century." The paper added:

> Indeed, the situation may be sufficiently dire that the civil service is experiencing what amounts to a 'quiet crisis' that if left unattended could produce major breakdowns in government performance in the future.

The indications that public service is not widely or highly valued by the present generation of college students are disturbing. Citing a Carnegie Commission study, the Levine-Kleeman paper pointed out that of the 1500 graduates in the Harvard class of 1985, only 3.3 percent planned to enter the federal government immediately. Still more discouraging was the finding of a career-path study by Harvard's Kennedy School of Government, where students are supposedly aiming for a career in government, that only 19.9 percent of graduates of the 2-year Master of Public Policy program work for the federal government, including Congress.

The public service is losing its attractions even for members of the Senior Executive Service. To find out why, the General Accounting Office sent a questionnaire last year to all the career executives who left the SES in fiscal 1985. Among more than 50 possible explanations for their decisions to leave, the 5 most often cited as of great or very great importance turned out to be: dissatisfaction with top management (cited by 47.3 percent), dissatisfaction with political appointees (the first reason restated—43.1 percent), unfair distribution of bonuses (41.4 percent), frustration with proposed and actual changes in compensation (39.9 percent), and frustration with criticism of federal workers by press, politicians or the public (36.9 percent).

Although dissatisfaction with salary and benefit levels was not ranked among the 10 most important reasons for leaving, my own guess is that the disparity between SES salaries and those of private-sector executives with equal or less responsibility was a bigger factor than the questionnaire revealed. In the case of officials covered by the Federal Salary Act, the gap between their salaries and corporate executives' pay has to have been demoralizing. In 1986 the Fifth Commission on Executive, Legislative and Judicial Salaries reported that the purchasing power of corporate executives' pay increased 68.5 percent between 1969 and 1984, more than doubling the gap between their pay and that of such federal executives as the Deputy Secretaries of State and Defense, the Chairman of the Federal Reserve Board, and the Administrator of NASA, who are at Level II of the pay scale. In 1969, the average corporate executive earned $140,000 or about three times the $42,000 earned by Level II Executives. By 1984, Level II pay had risen only to $72,600, while private executives averaged over *eight times* that amount.

In addition to declining in comparability, salaries governed by the Federal Salary Act also declined in purchasing power. From 1967 to 1985, the Consumer Price Index increased by more than 300%. The real income of most Americans, meanwhile, kept pace with inflation. During the same period the real income of top federal executives, legislators and judges fell by approximately 40 percent. Having entered the Nixon adminstration at Level II in 1969 and left the Carter administration at the same level in 1980, I know how they feel.

Additional damage has been done by the irresponsible rhetoric of political candidates who have run against "Washington." It would be hard to choose between Jimmy Carter and Ronald Reagan in this respect. In the words of Levine and Kleeman, the result has been "a growing perception among federal employees that they are unappreciated and underrewarded, which is affecting the morale and quality of the workforce at the entry level, among shortage groups, and at senior levels." The expected outcome is the "erosion of the human resource capacity of the federal workforce" to a degree that "raises a large question about what the future civil service will be like."

Despite these danger signals, there remain those who still insist that we have nothing to worry about. One of them is Terry W. Culler, Associate Director of the Office of Personnel Management in President Reagan's first term. In an article published by *The Wall Street Journal* in May, 1986, he contended that the government has no need for a workforce that is more than barely adequate to meet its minimum and routine requriements. "The government should be content," he wrote, "to hire competent people, not the best and most talented people." The "best and brightest," indeed, should not work in government at all, but should instead be channeled into the private sector where national wealth is created. I'm reminded of Senator Roman Hruska's justification of the Carswell nomination: there are a lot of mediocre people in this country, and they're entitled to be represented on the Supreme Court by a mediocre Justice.

The same complacent attitude is shared by all too many members of the business community. Lacking any real knowledge of how government works, they subscribe to the notion that the abler the government official, the more he or she will seek to enlarge the sphere of government at the expense of the private sector. To prevent this, they want the machinery of government placed in the hands of unambitious timeservers who will keep the wheels turning but can be counted on not to reach out for larger roles.

This simplistic view is, of course, diametrically opposed to the interests of business itself. As previously noted, superior talent and ability are needed to hold down the growth of big government. Mere competence will not insure that government programs fulfill their purposes with the least possible encroachment on the private sector. For this to be possible, the government decisionmaker, administrator or program designer must have a deeper understanding of the systemic relationships affected by government action than is needed if precision is not an object. Equally necessary is a sophisticated capacity to select from among a wide variety of tools—incentive devices, regulatory mechanisms, administrative procedures and the like—the one best suited to the task at hand.

To minimize the risk of undesired side-effects, government programs have to be designed and executed with knowledge and skill. Conversely, clumsiness, ignorance or indifference can lead to further intervention in order to correct the mistakes caused by the initial intervention. It is the defining characteristic of a system that if you put a strain on it anywhere, this strain will be transmitted throughout the whole; if you poke it in one place, it will bulge somewhere else. When you don't know just what will happen when you pull or poke, you're likely to have to find a remedy for an unintended effect. This in turn makes something else go wrong, and that too has to be corrected. The result can be like trying to even up the legs of a chair so that it will sit firmly on the floor: you take a little off one leg and then a little off another and another until you end up with a legless chair.

The more concerned you are, therefore, with protecting individual freedom and preserving private initiative, the more you should care about the quality of government. If government is to be kept from growing any faster than necessity demands and if programs that no longer serve an essential purpose are to be phased out, the people in charge have to be talented and smart. An ideological bias against big government is of less than no use. Indeed, all it does is get in the way of the understanding necessary to control big government. For one thing is certain: big government won't go away any sooner than the population of Philadelphia will revert to the 30,000 souls who lived there in 1787.

A second consequence of the mediocrity-is-sufficient fallacy is its tendency to undermine the relationship between political appointees and the career services. To succeed, this relationship requires effective cooperation and mutual respect between competent political managers who have a clear sense of what they want to accomplish and experienced bureaucrats who know how to get things done. Each group needs the other. If the former lack competence and/or a clear sense of direction, they cannot take full advantage of the latter's expertise. And if the career service is "sufficient" but not first-class, it cannot provide the quality of advice, program planning and follow-through necessary to the success of the administration's policies. Highly capable civil servants, in any case, could not by themselves, even if they wanted to, bring about the enlargement of the government's role: this kind of decision is not in their hands.

The trouble is that all too many political appointees enter government service without understanding any of the above. They suspect, instead, that senior civil servants lie awake at night scheming to sabotage the President's agenda and devising plans to promote their own. Having worked with most of the career services under five administrations, I can emphatically attest that this is not true. To the contrary, although many civil servants have ideas they are glad to put forward and would like to see adopted, they do not see themselves as performing a policymaking role. When approached with distrust, they respond with hostility, and the loser is the public interest.

Compounding all these negative influences on the career services are the increase in turnover and the decline in quality of second and third echelon political appointees. According to a recent study by the

National Academy of Public Administration, the tenure of Senate-confirmed appointees, which was 2.8 years under President Johnson, 2.6 years under President Nixon, and 2.5 years under President Carter, has dropped to 2 years under President Reagan. One result is that the tour of duty of a given appointee seldom overlaps for more than a few months with the tours of the other non-career people with whom he works. There has been a drop, meanwhile, in the experience level of political appointees with respect both to government generally and to their agency's field of responsibility. A contributing factor, no doubt, has been the elimination from the pool of eligible prospects of those who cannot meet the prescribed ideological litmus test.

As if all this weren't bad enough, more and more political appointees are being pushed into jobs traditionally held by career officials. In addition to reducing the number of positions at the top that remain open to a civil servant, the consequence is to place minimally qualified individuals in highly important posts. It's hard enough to get really good people to give up highly paid positions in private life and take on the demanding duties of an under secretary or assistant secretary; it's harder still to persuade an able and experienced person to accept the less prestigious title of deputy assistant secretary. Almost any job at that level, however, is more responsible and has wider impact on the national interest than most senior corporate positions. In the State Department, for example, a deputy assistant secretary is responsible for all of Southeast Asia. In the Commerce Department, a deputy assistant secretary is in charge of export controls. A deputy assistant attorney general heads the war against organized crime. Comparable responsibilities belong to every similar position throughout the federal government.

Ignoring these facts, patronage offices pressed to come up with jobs for the President's loyal supporters drive the politicizing process. A White House personnel assistant sees the position of deputy assistant secretary as a fourth-echelon slot. In his eyes that makes it an ideal reward for a fourth-echelon political type—a campaign advance man, for instance, or a regional political organizer. For a senior civil servant, on the other hand, it's irksome to see a position one has spent twenty or thirty years preparing for preempted by an outsider who doesn't know the difference between an audit exception and an authorizing bill. Small wonder, then, that so many members of the SES have sought other occupations.

To correct these trends will not be easy. Last year's Brookings-AEI conference focused on a broad array of possible remedies. Among those discussed were more flexibility in creating special categories of personnel eligible for higher pay, higher priority for the development of managers, the reversion of responsibility for personnel management from an office headed by a single director to an independent Commission, better orientation and briefing of political appointees, and the removal of impediments to the recruitment of young people into federal agencies. Reform, however, is not enough. The crisis in the public service can be dispelled only by fundamental changes of attitude on the part of political leaders, the business community, and the general public. A sustained and powerful appeal, moreover, must be directed toward young people approaching a career choice.

On the political front, it's important to reach the Presidential candidates and their staffs between now and the 1988 Conventions, and the President-elect should be approached again during the transition period. An attempt should also be made to get the major parties to address the issue in their platforms. Tomorrow's politicians must be made to feel that "Washington-bashing" is wrong, counterproductive and old hat. Beyond that, the next administration's most valuable contribution to restoring pride in public service and zest for its performance would be to join a clear sense of direction with the conviction that government can be a positive force.

As to the business community, the essential point to be communicated is that the private sector's freedom depends on the public sector's quality. As much or more than any other element of the society, business has a stake in assuring that government gets its share of the best and brightest. It is crucial to get this across to those business executives who instinctively distrust any bureaucracy but their own.

Changing the public perception of government service cannot be accomplished, of course, without the help of the media. They will have to be convinced of the newsworthiness as well as the merit of the cause. This will require from those of us already convinced of the latter a concerted effort to dig out the facts that explain the present trends and find new ways of dramatizing the seriousness of their impact. Unless the crisis ceases to be "quiet" it will continue to be chronic.

For the media themselves, the crisis creates an opportunity. As we have been reminded by the recent Bicentennial of the Constitution, in areas where we the people have not made government our surrogate we have relied on those most directly concerned to take proper account of the public interest. The publication of news and opinions is not only such an area but one that also enjoys affirmative protection. Thus insulated from any enforceable obligation to serve the public interest, the media can fairly be asked to have special concern for government's capacity to do so. It would be helpful if, in addition to highlighting needed improvements, they could also, from time to time, call attention to things that have been done right.

Young people's perception of the attractiveness (or otherwise) of a government career will, of course, be influenced by political leaders as well as the media. Educational institutions reach young people more directly. They should be trying harder to make students aware both of the rewards and satisfactions of public service and of the avenues by which it can be pursued. When I talk with students, I tell them that what you do in government at any given level matters more than what business people at a comparable level do. What *they* do is good for the management and the stockholders, and some-times—if they're lucky—for the customers as well. What *you* do affects the well-being—the survival even—of millions.

I also stress the importance of how you feel about what you do. If you're working for the public, your only concern is, or should be, doing your best within the sphere entrusted to you to discern and carry out the course of action that will best serve the interests of your fellow citizens. To know that that's your job is a good feeling. As Paul Volcker said at the final meeting of the Brookings-AEI conference:

> For all the glories of Adam Smith, somebody has to set the rules and adjudicate disputes. Somebody has to defend the country and to explore space. Somebody has to keep the air clean and the environment safe for the next generation. Somebody has to respond to those more mundane, but nonetheless sometimes quite challenging assignments of keeping government working effectively and efficiently, if self-government is to work at all.
>
> I would think that it is true today as it ever was that there should be immense satisfaction in doing any one of those things. . . . There is still a certain satisfaction that your only client is the United States government—the American people—and not a particular interest . . . there is still a special excitement in directly contributing to policy rather than commenting about it.

I have many friends who once held responsible but not necessarily prominent roles in government and who now occupy prestigious and well-paid positions in the private sector—some of them *very* prestigious and *very* well-paid. The kind of satisfaction Paul Volcker talks about is still very real to them. Not one finds his present occupation as rewarding as his government service. If they feel this way, so must a lot of others, and that could explain why business executives are paid so much more than their government counterparts. Society treats public servants, together with teachers, ministers, and the practitioners of certain other honorable but low-paid callings, as the beneficiaries of a high level of psychic income. It would seem that society does not attribute comparable satisfaction to corporate servitude.

The effort to mobilize broad-based support for a concerted attack on the problems of the public service now has a new protagonist. This is the newly formed National Commission on the Public Service which Paul Volcker has agreed to head. As recently announced, the Commission's objectives include building public awareness of the essentiality of the career services to carrying out the national agenda, promoting measures for strengthening the morale and efficiency of government employees at all levels, encouraging the pursuit of excellence by government workers themselves, and making government a more attractive and accessible career choice for young people. Working closely with Congress and other organizations, schools, and centers concerned with the quality of the public service, the Commission will tackle these objectives over a two-year period. As one of its organizers, I have high hopes for its contribution to strengthening government's ability to respond to the ever more difficult demands that the years ahead are sure to place upon it.

One final thought. In an address to the Virginia Convention that ratified the Constitution, James Madison declared, "I go on this great republican principle, that the people will have virtue and intelligence to select men of virtue and wisdom." For two hundred years we the people of America have justified this faith. So too, by and large, have those whom we selected and those whom they appointed. The task of making sure that Madison's great principle will continue to be fulfilled rests where it always has—in our hands.

Return to Women's Rights

Representative Bill Green

In an August 1987 nationally syndicated column, David S. Broder asked the question, "Can a Feminist Be a Republican?" The answer I gave in a subsequent op-ed piece was "Yes, He/She Can." A feminist believes in and works for political, economic and social equality of the sexes. I have found during my years as an elected official, both at the state and federal levels, that a Republican can be committed to the concept and practical application of this principle for this is not at odds with the *traditional* role of the party. True, with party leaders now embracing a more conservative credo, it has been more difficult to advance the feminist cause. But I believe that this is a temporary condition. There are reasons for moderate Republicans to remain vocal and active feminists.

WHERE WE WERE

Were there eyebrows raised at the word "traditional?" The Grand Old Party actually had a pretty decent record on women's rights. The Republican Party called for "equal pay for equal work" as early as 1896. By 1916 the party was giving grudging support for a woman's right to vote and its platform said that "as a measure of justice . . . [it] favors the extension of the suffrage to women, but recognizes the right of each state to settle this question itself." Well, this was ducking the issue a bit. Sounds like some Republicans' position on the Equal Rights Amendment (ERA) today.

But then in 1919, it was a Republican Congress that proposed the 19th Amendment! A year later, with women's suffrage on the near horizon, the platform said that: "We earnestly hope the Republican legislatures in states which have not yet acted on the Suffrage Amendment will ratify the amendment . . . which is so important to the welfare of our country." And, in fact, the Republican-controlled state legislatures did that—of the 36 states that ratified, 29 were GOP-controlled.

In 1923, Republicans Charles Curtis and Daniel Anthony—nephew of the suffragette Susan B. Anthony—submitted an equal rights amendment in the Congress. In 1940, the ERA was endorsed by the party. In 1952, the GOP platform stated that: "We recommend to Congress the submission of a constitutional amendment providing equal rights for men and women," and also said "We favor legislation assuring equal pay for equal work regardless of sex."

The Democratic Party platform support for equal rights came in somewhat later and it carried the pledges less often over the decades, possibly due in part to the opposition of organized labor.

I will let others evaluate why the ERA sat relatively dormant so long—as words rather than actions—but I think we can assume that activity was spurred in recent years because of economic necessity and because women, as a result of better birth control methods and the movement to smaller families, gained the freedom to make decisions about child bearing and thus about entering, or remaining within, the workplace.

WHERE WE ARE

Why should the Republican Party care about this history? Because the party is not so popular with the public that it can turn away voters who believe in equality for women.

The 1980 and 1984 White House races were victories for Ronald Reagan more than for the GOP. And despite the assumption in some quarters that the first Reagan victory spelled a hard shift to the right, Republican voters tend to inhabit the center. Indicative of this were the 1980 primaries results through April of that year, before candidates began to drop out. Through the early primaries, the more moderate candidates, Anderson, Baker and Bush, were pulling down slightly more than 50 percent of the vote! Reagan dominated the race because while the moderates shared their half, he was getting almost all of the rest.

Another indication that the party cannot assume widespread and deep popularity is the fact that for decades it has been a minority in the House, it lost the Senate after just a brief period of control and it is not doing too well with state houses. And while more people are calling themselves Republican and "conservative" than a decade ago, the term Republican is still only chosen by 30 percent of the electorate compared to 40 percent for Democrats and an impressive 30 percent as "independents."

Clearly voters are there for the taking by the party or politicians that offer the right programs and advance popular policies. What type of policies? Well, as a former member of the Eisenhower administration once noted: "In politics, as in chess, whoever holds the center holds a position of almost unbeatable strength."

Where is the center? Much has been written about the economic conservatism of the "yuppies" and still younger people. Indeed, the economic turnabout since the dreary Carter years was a major asset for Reagan, especially among those who appreciated the tax cuts and the strong drop in inflation and interest rates. But even in relatively good times voters do consider non-monetary matters issues and the perception of the health of the US economy can change quickly (see October 19, 1987, "Black Monday" on the stock market). It would be foolish indeed for the party to assume it can rely on this one issue.

Published polls have shown over recent years that while the "yuppies" like tax cuts, they also either oppose cuts, or support increases in spending for social programs. They support arms control, generally favor freedom of choice on abortion, back equality of women in education and the workforce and demand a clean environment.

And what of the following generation? While studies of the 18–25 age group showed that financial success seems to be their top interest, and while the GOP has done well with this group, non-conservative attitudes on social issues remain. The survey of college freshmen done by the University of California at Los Angeles American Council on Education reported that 35 percent of this group called themselves "Republican," 23 percent said they were "Democratic" and a sizable 36 percent chose "Independent." But, the survey warned, this did not mean the frosh are conservative. As quoted in the *Washington Post*, the Council said that a change in attitudes since the mid '60s "has not been from liberal to conservative, but from left to center."

And while the number callilng themselves "liberal" has dropped, the number calling themselves "middle-of-the-road" has surged.

The Republican Party already is experiencing negative effects for its movement away from its progressive roots on social issues. In the 1984 elections, in only one of 23 Senate races analyzed by pundits did a Republican appeal more to women than to men. That was Senator Bob Packwood of Oregon, who has a strong record of supporting women's rights issues. In North Carolina, Republican James Broyhill carried the men's vote but lost the women's and the race. In a tight race in North Dakota, women provided the edge for the Democrat. According to some evaluations, the "gender gap" cost the GOP up to seven Senate races. Losing women lost Republicans the Senate. Let me suggest that the reason for this is that a vocal segment of the Republican Party is ignoring not only the party's traditional view but also the public's contemporary views.

ISSUES

For example, a majority of American adults, including 65% of women, support the Equal Rights Amendment. Yet, in 1980 after forty years of support, social conservatives in control of the platform had it dropped. Absurd. I do not think that the party can be held responsible for the failure of the ERA to be adopted by a sufficient number of state legislatures. There was effective if not always honest lobbying by opponents and some ERA advocates undoubtedly caused their effort real harm when they allied themselves with the Democratic Party—it is difficult if not impossible to obtain the support of both houses of Congress and three-quarters of the state legislatures if one takes a highly partisan position. Yet even if the ERA itself is sidetracked, the underlying issue of equality for women remains active.

Abortion is perhaps the most contentious issue in this country and all moderates do not agree on the issue. But the Supreme Court has ruled that choice is a woman's right. That is the *law*. And consider the views of the majority of Americans as shown by a variety of professional polls.

• A large majority of adults, including 72% of women, support some degree of freedom of choice.

• While some feel abortion should be permitted only under certain circumstances, a majority (54%) believe it should be permitted no matter what the reason.

• A large majority (77%) believe that abortion will remain legal.

• A majority (55%) know someone who has had an abortion.

• Large majorities (87% and 88% respectively) believe that if abortions were made illegal, women would get illegal abortions and many would be physically harmed as a result.

• Between 1978 and 1986, 21 states or localities had referenda against abortion. Twenty failed.

Yet the party's official position, as put forth by the Reagan administration and in the 1984 platform, is opposition to a woman's right to choose, going so far as to seek to select federal judges according to their views on this issue. In Congress, amendments to legislation and appropriation bills have denied many women (federal employees, Peace Corps workers, Native Americans, women on Medicaid) the right to use their medical insurance to pay for abortions. It would seem appropriate for the party to recognize legitimate differences in opinion on this difficult issue, rather than try to restrict what are the legal rights of women.

This leads us right into family planning. It would appear that social conservatives in the party would like to see every form of family planning disappear. Some attack basic birth control. (Presidential candidate Pat Robertson preached that we need larger families and a bigger population!) In their zeal to prevent legal abortions, the social conservatives are seeking to squeeze out family planning services internationally and domestically. The latest move by the Reagan administration is to propose regulatory changes to prohibit medical personnel and counselors in federally-funded (Title X) programs from simply *informing* patients that abortion is one of a variety of choices or, and this to me is amazing, even responding to a patient's request for information! Indeed, it patently conflicts with the ethical obligation to obtain "informed consent" from the patient for the course of medical care prescribed.

This extreme position is not anti-abortion, it is a demand that medical ethics and free speech rights be ignored. If the party and its leaders allow themselves to be pushed into such positions, we shall find ourselves isolated from the mainstream of American opinion and probably out ofjobs. Such positions also are ironic, as the Title X program came into being during a Republican administration and has had strong bi-partisan support in Congress for years. Furthermore, as family planning services, including contraception, are denied, more unwanted pregnancies will occur and thus more abortions will be sought. This will place the social archconservatives in the position of advancing what they most abhor. Not only is this illogical, it is cruel and hardly likely to gain the support of most Americans.

Again, one must respect the beliefs of individual office holders and citizens, but clearly in the case of choice and family planning, a minority position has captured the party, to some extent because anti-abortionists can be one-issue voters but also because they have gained undue influence on the party's mechanisms and leadership.

The ability of women to obtain full family planning services affects their ability to enter and remain in the work force. Again, while many conservatives view the working woman as non-traditional, history shows otherwise. In early 1987, a research organization, the Batelle Memorial Institute, released a report on "The Changing Course of American Women" for the Hearst Corporation. One interesting fact in the report is that the stereotype of a woman only leaving her parent's home to get married and have children is based not upon a long history, but upon one atypical generation: the post-WWII experience.

In many ways, today's women, electing for education equal to that of men, substantial work experience, delayed marriage and both delayed and limited childbearing, reflects her grandmother and great-grandmother's experience and desires.

Polling of teenage women today shows that the vast majority expect to have careers throughout their adulthood—while also choosing to be married and have children. There clearly is no reason to expect a reversal of this in the future, and so society and government need to accept this new/old role of women, and to plan and react accordingly. Political/governmental decisions on issues affecting education, the work environment, retirement and the like will have to be based on the fact that what is called the "primary woman," one with her own plans and activities, is back to stay.

According to *Workforce 2000*, a report by the Hudson Institute, 61 percent of married women and 52 percent of women with children under the age of six currently perform work for pay. This compares to just 11 percent in 1960. By the turn of the century, approximately 47 percent of the U.S. workforce will be women and 60% of all adult women will be workers. In fact, between 1985 and 2000 women are expected to make up about 60 percent of the new workforce entrants.

A potential problem for the Republican party is that some lawmakers and business people appear unwilling to recognize the growth and permanence of the working woman and the two-wage earner family. Congress is considering legislation to permit workers to take unpaid leave for childbirth or to care for a sick child or parent. It hardly is a radical idea since most European countries already have such provisions and in many cases they provide *paid* leave under such circumstances. This legislation provides an opportunity for the party to be responsive to a situation that, while affecting both genders, realistically impacts more upon women. Fortunately, some Republicans joined in a bipartisan compromise in the House that protected small companies from hardships while still advancing the concept that business must recognize that the worker is also a member of a family!

There is little doubt in my mind that this or similar legislation will become law in the near future. There is also little doubt that voters will approve of such action. The only question is whether Republicans as a group will be on the winning/popular side.

Despite the numbers of working women, poverty in this country is still substantially a women-and-child problem. In 1985, women headed more than 48 percent of poor households. Thus any discussion of women's issues must include welfare reform. In 1935, when the Aid to Families with Dependent Children (AFDC) program began with the aim of helping widowed women with children, the popular wisdom was that mothers would/should be home full-time and the program reflected that. By 1987, the scenario had radically changed. The AFDC rolls are swelled with single, never married mothers who more often than not remain on the rolls for a decade. This long dependency puts both mother and children in a weak position to achieve self-sufficency. That, together with the rise in the number of working mothers, is forcing policy makers to rethink the way we design welfare programs. Moderate Republicans must take part in the discussion and help design a resolution that acknowledges what women are today, not what some people think they should be.

No, it is not easy right now to be both a feminist and a Republican. But that does not mean we have to choose between our party and our feminist beliefs. It does mean that a lot of hard work needs to be done to bring the moderate element back to the forefront of the Republican Party. And as one who tried unsuccessfully to round up enough state delegations to challenge the party's lack of an ERA plank at the 1980 convention, and who has been lobbying to have the party at least neutral on "choice," I know how difficult the battle can be. I do not suggest that all Republicans must have the same views on all the issues. Certainly, any major party needs to be open to different views. But to be a true majority party, the Republican Party must be in step with the majority of Americans, and that includes American women.

Where the party clearly has been out of step is in its platform. Archconservatives have gained control and it is imperative that moderates work to try to take conservative "litmus tests" out of that document. Where there are clear differences of opinion within the party, such as on abortion, the platform should not try to exclude substantial numbers of office holders and a millions of the rank-and-file. In other areas it must recognize that we cannot ignore the role and rights of women. Some moderates in Congress are attempting to deal with these issues in the 1988 platform and grassroots efforts will be necessary to get moderates deeply involved for 1992 and beyond.

While some may claim that "nobody reads a platform," the fact is that our opponents and women's rights organizations do so and negative planks are used to bang local moderate Republican candidates over the head during elections. Perhaps I would not mind this so much if these nay-sayers were just sitting quietly on their back porches grumbling about a world they do not understand. But instead they are thwarting the desires of a large minority of our population, denying the rights of women, and damning our party to a minority status in government. For in the case of women's rights, political officials and organizations have to realize that women MUST be granted their right to choose their economic and social roles. True, it has been a long time developing, but it is going to happen.

If one were to walk along the rocky shoreline of Maine or of Northern California and watch the waves pound at the rocks, you would not discern any erosion. But you know it is happening. And you know that eventually, inevitably, the waves will crumble any resistance. So it is with equal rights for women. It will win out, as it should. Any political group that fails to accept and support this will be condemned to be a minority in government and to a loss of leadership in society.

Progressive Republicans have three jobs to do: first, we have to make it clear to the public that the party is not of one voice on these issues—that a goodly number of us are pro-ERA, pro women's rights in general. We have to stop allowing the "anti" forces to dominate the microphones, headlines and podiums.

Second, we have to work to elect more progressives. I know we are not clones, we have different views on some issues, but we are sufficiently akin to work together and return the Republican Party to the political center where the people live.

Third, the national Republican leadership must recognize the legitimate demands of the American public not only on women's rights but in areas such as civil rights, the environment, consumerism and other programs. If the party does not respond to those demands, does not return to its progrssive traditions, then it will continue to be a minority in Congress and in our political society. If it does respond, while still keeping its ability to forego short-term "political hay-making" in favor of long-term benefits for the nation, then the public, in its growing sophistication, will show its approval and a strong two-party system will remain.

There are hurdles: moderates, by definition, tend to avoid extreme positions which attract public (and press) attention. Moderates of both parties also tend, to their credit, to spend their time on the nuts and bolts of the legislative/governmental process. As one complained at a small gathering in my office, "While we [Republican moderates] are working with the Democratic moderates on legislation, the conservatives are up making speeches."

But while moderates have some quiet influence on specific and immediate issues, they are not defining the future roles of government or the party. They are not attracting the attention of the public, whose support they need to gain the power to influence party philosophy, and thus government action.

If Republican moderates fail to take decisive action, we will remain a minority in the party, the GOP will lose support among the voters, and the voters will lose a viable alternative to the more moderate Democratic Party we should expect to see in the future. The existence of two competing centrist parties has been an integral part of our democracy, and for either party to depend upon one political "wing" is not in anyone's best interest. It is up to us to see that our party understands and heeds this fact.

Reconciling Conflicting Values to Preserve Individual Dignity and Liberty

Donald T. Bliss

The character of America's commitment to liberty is rooted in the special way the nation was conceived and populated. With the stark exception of native Americans and most black Americans, people came to this country from all over the world in search of individual dignity or economic opportunity. They came from diverse cultural, economic and political environments. They did not come with any inherent tolerance for other points of view. But the sheer complexity of creating a workable social fabric out of such diverse cultural strands compelled the development of legal rules that foster mutual respect and tolerance. The tension in any democracy between majority rule and the protection of minority rights was eased by the fact that the majority itself consisted of so many ethnic and religious minorities.

Further, the nation itself was conceived to preserve the people's "inalienable rights" of "life, liberty, and the pursuit of happiness." By these words, independence was declared and a new concept of government premised on respect for individual dignity and liberty was created. The Constitution itself did little to elaborate upon that premise; indeed, it reflected the arcane views of the era on race, sex and economic status, but it did provide for a government based on laws, a system of checks and balances, and a limited federal mandate of specifically enumerated powers. This structure would greatly inhibit any intrusion by the national government into personal liberties.

Moreover, as the price of ratification, the Constitution was quickly amended, and the Bill of Rights expressed in mostly general terms the promise of a free society. Some of the freedoms—religion, speech, and free press—were so central to the conception of the new nation that they were deeply ingrained in the legal system from the start, although they have been refined and broadened to meet changing circumstances.

In other instances, it took the Civil War and additional constitutional amendments to provide a framework within which liberty for all Americans became a possibility. The Thirteenth Amendment abolished slavery. The Fourteenth Amendment expanded the principles of due process and equal protection under the law. The Fifteenth Amendment guaranteed the right to vote regardless of race.

Most recently there has been increasing recognition of the right to privacy implicit in the constitutional amendments. The right to privacy is implicit in the First, Third, Fourth, Fifth and Fourteenth Amendments to the Constitution, and possibly the Ninth ("The enumeration in the Constitution of certain rights, shall not be construed to deny or disparage others retained by the people.") and the Tenth (powers not delegated to the United States. . . . "are reserved to the States, respectively, or the people."). Privacy is so central to the founding premise of individual dignity and liberty that any attempt to define it precisely would have served only to constrain its essential function in preserving minority values in a system of majority rule. External manifestations of private views or activities that may impinge on the interests of others or the state are expressly protected, *e.g.*, freedom of speech and assembly and freedom from unreasonable search and seizure. Thus, the exercise of free speech articulating private values may intrude on the rights of others and is expressly protected, but the right to hold certain beliefs or engage in certain activities that have no consequence beyond the privacy of one's home conflicts with no one but a meddling, intrusive government, or a government seeking to impose the majority's values on a minority of dissenters.

In realizing the founding fathers' promise of a government based on respect for individual dignity and liberty and in creating a legal structure that extends that promise to all Americans, by far the greatest progress has been made within the past thirty years. Because for so many Americans the gap between the promise and the reality had been so great during most of our history, great progress could be made by simply eliminating gross injustices sanctioned by government, *e.g.*, racial segregation of the schools, deprivation of the criminal defendant's right to counsel, restricting the right to vote through poll taxes, literacy tests, etc. In recent decades, all three branches of the federal government have contributed to the development of laws that have narrowed the gap. Congress passed significant civil rights, voting rights, and fair housing legislation, among others. The Supreme Court issued such landmark decisions as *Brown v. Board of Education* (desegregating public schools), *Gideon v. Wainwright* (right to counsel), and *Griswold v. Connecticut* (invalidating anti-birth control statues as an invasion of privacy). The Executive Branch courageously enforced the law as symbolized by the actions of Presidents Eisenhower and Kennedy on school desegregation at Little Rock and the University of Alabama.

Uncomfortable with the proliferation of legal rights and remedies over the past thirty years, some feel that the pendulum has swung too far and that the nation now faces a period of retrenchment, if not regression, as the pendulum swings back. However, while the basic legal framework for preserving civil liberties and rights is largely— although not completely—in place, the practical economic and social realization of a society committed to liberty and individual dignity for all Americans is far from complete. It will require vigilant effort simply to sustain the progress that has been made. In the face of new complexities, making further progress over the next thirty years will be even more challenging as the following four considerations illustrate.

First, pursuing further progress through the legal system increasingly will result in a clash of rights and values that must be reconciled. Instead of simply eliminating gross injustices, government will be asked to preserve, advance or create specific rights and remedies in ways that intrude on other important and compelling civil liberties, rights and values. Often there will not be any single libertarian point of view, and rigid adherence to conventional positions will obscure the importance of emerging values that must be recognized, weighed and compared. That some of these values are not constitutionally protected does not make them less worthy of recognition and preservation. For example, in addition to the rights of criminal defendants, there is increasing recognition that victims and potential victims of crime also have rights. In addition to the rights of parents to decide whether to have children and how to raise them, there is increasing recognition that children also have rights to a safe, abuse-free and healthy life.

In resolving these conflicts, there are no absolutes or fixed constitutional formulae. Each set of circumstances must be resolved on the facts presented. The rights at stake must be articulated, weighed and compared. In some instances, conflicting rights may be reconciled in a way that does the least damage to each. In other cases, certain rights must be preserved at the expense of others either because they are constitutionally protected or because they are appropriate for government intervention. In the resolution of such conflicts, the roles performed by the legislative, judicial, and executive branches differ greatly, but they share a common commitment to constitutional principles, expressed and implicit. Foremost among these principles is the government's respect for individual dignity, freedom of belief and expression, and tolerance of diversity. Equally as important is the government's recognition that its role in defining rights and choosing among them is strictly limited and confined mostly to process. Its role is to protect the right of free speech, not to evaluate its content. Its role is to ensure the criminal defendant's right to a fair trial, not to measure fairness by the gravity of the offense. Its role is to protect individuals from physical injury and abuse, not to determine the extent and nature of appropriate health care.

In the first example cited above, comparing the rights of the criminal and those of the victim, the right not to be deprived of life and liberty without due process of law is so fundamental to a free society, and in the case of criminal suspects, so clearly expressed in the constitutional amendments, that society must bear the risk to innocent victims inherent in the preservation of this right. Admittedly, certain guilty persons will go free and certain crimes will be committed while a defendant is accorded a fair trial. Like soldiers who die on a battlefield defending liberty, this is a price that must be paid to prevent an erosion of the safeguards all Americans enjoy against the abuses of the state's police powers. But the right is not absolute. In certain circumstances, such as the setting or denying of bail, compelling evidence of specific danger to the life of an innocent third party would justify incarceration until due process is expeditiously accomplished.

In the second example cited above, the rights of parents to decide whether to have children and how to raise them is as fundamental a liberty as any expressly recognized in the constitutional amendments.

The government's obligation is to protect the exercise of this liberty and not to intrude upon it or to substitute the state's values for those of the parent. But this right is not absolute. Parents cannot be allowed to abuse their children physically or to neglect altogether their children's right to an education that will enable them to realize their own potential for individual dignity. Beyond ensuring these basic rights, however, the government has no role. Consistent with the preservation of individual liberty, government should not dictate to parents the kind of education their children must have or the type of health care they must provide. Under the guise of protecting the "rights" of children, government should not impose on parents the majority's views about what constitutes adequate education or health care, however noble the objective, since the cost to individual freedom, tolerance of minority values and diversity is simply too great a price to pay.

A second illustration of the challenge to preserving individual liberty and dignity involves advances in technology, particularly in the biomedical and computer sciences, which will strain severely government's ability to use information wisely and in ways that adequately safeguard individual privacy. The ability to predict diseases based on genetic analysis, for example, will create countless opportunities for discrimination in jobs, insurance coverage, and even with respect to such fundamental values as the right to marry and bear children. Protecting the privacy of such information goes to the very core of our society's commitment to preserving individual dignity without intrusive government intervention. But the pressure for access to such information will be tremendous as other competing values are asserted, including the rights of prospective spouses and unborn children, the rights of the insured to reasonable premiums based on known risks, the rights of airline passengers to safe transportation in the hands of healthy pilots, and so on.

Given the inevitable gap between science's capacity to diagnose and its ability to prevent or cure disease, it is probable that the debate today over the use of AIDS testing represents only the tip of the iceberg. While protecting the confidentiality of AIDS tests results is essential to preserve privacy and prevent disrimination—and also is necessary if a testing program is to work at all—society cannot ignore the rights of third parties to be safe from infection. Since the AIDS virus has no respect for state boundaries, federal legislation is needed to ensure confidentiality and prevent discrimination. Where a physician learns, however, that an infected person is exposing another party to possible infection and cannot be persuaded to inform that party that he or she has tested positive, the physician should be authorized to inform such party.

Third, as equality under the law becomes a reality it will become increasingly apparent that economic disparities preclude for many the realization of the American promise. This will intensify the conflict between competing rights as the issue becomes how to allocate the costs of improving economic opportunities for persons or classes of persons subject to past discrimination or who, for whatever reason, are unable to share in the benefits of a free society. For example, children in economically deprived areas may receive an inferior education because the low tax base allocates far fewer funds than are available to public schools in wealthy districts. Is there a fundamental right to a quality education? If so, must local school financing be equalized to ensure that poor children are not deprived of this right? A basic education clearly is essential to participate fully in the benefits of a free society. While absolute equality of educational opportunity is neither desirable nor obtainable, the right to a good elementary and secondary education is essential to the concept of individual dignity and the proper functioning of democratic govern- ment. Educational funds must be allocated in ways which assure that such rights are not denied to children for reasons of geographic location or economic status.

Finally, as more comprehensive laws against discrimination have been enacted, the nature of the problems they address have changed. Discrimination on the basis of race, sex, handicap, ethnic origins or sexual preference has become less overt, more subtle, but often just as persistent. Extending the law to reach these less tangible manifes- tations of discrimination may intrude too deeply into areas of private activity and conflict with other rights, which also must be accorded respect. Can a private employer consider sexual preference or handi- cap in selecting household employees? May a church hire for secular jobs only persons who share its religious convictions? Eliminating subtle patterns of discrimination from the nation's social fabric will require more than a resort to law. It will require innovative ap- proaches to educate, persuade and encourage people to respect and value the rights of others.

Continuing the nation's commitment to individual liberty and dignity over the next thirty years often will require comparing and reconciling competing rights and interests. As new rights are created, and old rights more broadly defined and expanded, these conflicts will increase. Resolving these conflicts is not always a question of comparing the interests at stake and choosing the more important one. It requires a clear definition of the rights to be protected and values to be preserved, and then often an innovative approach to accommodating each of the values to the greatest extent possible. Constitutional principles establish the priorities and guide the analysis. To limit constitutional analysis, however, to ascertaining the original intent or to the prohibitions of specific language, as some have suggested, would badly cripple the process of relevant reconciliation. Reconciliation based on constitutional analysis can be effective only if rights are defined in a concrete, current context, and constitutional principles applied to real world circumstances today.

Not all values worthy of preservation are constitutionally protected rights, but they may be important nonetheless. The following examples illustrate how the preservation of freedom and maximization of individual liberty for all Americans often requires the reconciliation of competing values.

1. Freedom of the Press vs. Freedom From Malicious Libel

Freedom of the press is the ultimate guarantor of individual dignity because it provides the information by which the people can participate responsibly in the democratic process and ultimately exercise control over their government. As Justice Black, who believed this freedom to be absolute, wrote in *Mills v. Alabama:*

> The Constitution specifically selected the press . . . to play an important role in the discussion of public affairs. Thus, the press serves and was designed to serve, as a powerful anecdote to any abuse of power by government officials and as a constitutionally chosen means for keeping officials elected by the people responsive to all the people whom they are selected to serve.

Moreover, the press is the very means by which information essential to the functioning of government must flow unfettered. As Justice Powell stated in *Saxby v. Washington Post Company*, the press:

> . . . is the means by which people receive that free flow of information and ideas essential to intelligent self-government.

Yet, a free press also can destroy individual dignity as quickly and completely as any abuse of the state's police power. What constraints should there be on the abuse of the press, particularly if that abuse maliciously deprives a person of his or her livelihood and reputation? Good people may be deterred from seeking public office because they are unwilling to accept such a burden or impose it on their families. The government itself is held accountable through elections and a system of checks and balances. But who checks the abusive press? In a nation dedicated to preserving the value of individual dignity against governmental oppression, should there not be some protection against oppression by the press? Certainly, government cannot provide it.

One of the few restraints on the press is the threat of libel suits and damages for injuries to reputation caused by the spreading of false information. Yet even this threat, enforced through the judiciary, can have a chilling effect on the ability of the press to ferret out information essential to a free society.

Over twenty years ago in *New York Times v. Sullivan*, the Supreme Court attempted to reconcile these competing values by recognizing the special role of the press in our constitutional system and requiring that the press be accorded some margin of error since otherwise the fear of error in commenting on public officials could discourage the press from vigorously pursuing the truth. The Court established an "actual malice" test, stating that public officials claiming libel must show that a libelous statement was made "with knowledge that it was false or with reckless disregard of whether it was false or not." The *Sullivan* decision thus establishes a higher standard for public officials, presumably because in accepting positions of responsibility they accept the greater risk inherent in public life.

Experience with the *Sullivan* test has not been entirely satisfactory. On the one hand, it has not prevented the press from imposing severe damage to personal reputations, in some instances based on false information. On the other hand, it has not prevented the proliferation of libel suits. Seeking to prove "actual malice," offended parties have engaged in extensive discovery of documents, conversations and confidential sources in order to shed some light on press motivation. This has had a chilling effect on the willingness of the press to seek out facts necessary to hold government accountable.

In the end, as the founding fathers foresaw, the press is so vital to the proper functioning of democratic government that its powers must be near absolute when the scrutiny of public officials and public issues is at stake. Today, since the issues addressed by government are far more complex and the potential for abuse of power is far greater, the role of the press is even more vital. Thus, the *Sullivan* principle, which affords a greater measure of press freedom in matters involving public officials and issues, must be preserved. But public officials should not be asked to relinquish their basic liberties when they run for office. The malice test thus provides a necessary check. It would be better, however, if it were applied in a way that did not encourage the proliferation of libel suits and extensive discovery requests. This can be avoided if the press itself establishes a voluntary, nonjudicial means to ascertain the truthfulness of press accounts and to provide for remedies where false information is disseminated. Such remedies would include both prominently displayed corrections and monetary damages.

2. Personal Privacy vs. Personal Safety

The U.S. Department of Transportation recently ordered random drug testing for certain transportation employees performing safety-related responsibilities. When there is no particularized suspicion that a specific employee has taken drugs, such random testing may constitute an invasion of his or her personal privacy in contravention of the Fourth Amendment which bars unreasonable searches and seizures without probable cause.

On the other hand, the passenger presumably is entitled to safe transportation which surely must include an expectation that an air traffic controller or the operator of an airplane, train or bus is not under the influence of drugs. Such an expectation may override the employee's reasonable expectation of privacy in his or her choice of occupation.

Can these important conflicting values be reconciled? Since random testing represents an intrusion into individual privacy that, once taken, is difficult to retract, it is essential that this step not be taken as some kind of faddish response to the public perception of a generalized "safety" problem. Where this is a clearly demonstrated need based on specific factual evidence, however, such testing may be appropriate for employees in certain safety-related positions, *e.g.*, pilots, train engineers and bus drivers, under circumstances where drug impairment could endanger the lives of third parties.

A constitutionally sustainable drug testing program for this limited class of employees, however, must meet certain standards, as follows: (1) there is convincing evidence that drug use is a problem for the particular class of employees and that the use of drugs by those employees would present a threat to life and safety; (2) other forms of testing, *e.g.*, pre-employment screening, post-accident testing, or testing based on individualized suspicion, are inadequate to meet demonstrated safety needs; (3) random testing is a part of a written drug testing policy of which the employee has advance notice; (4) there are safeguards to ensure personal privacy in taking the test and the confidentiality of the test results; (5) the tests are performed by an accredited laboratory that meets the highest standards of accuracy and an initial positive test is subject to a second confirmatory test; (6) there is a process by which the employee can challenge the test results and seek an independent medical review; (7) the test results cannot be used for any purpose unrelated to transportation safety, *e.g.*, they cannot be used to prosecute the employee for drug use; (8) an employee may not be terminated on the basis of a single incident and must be accorded counseling and rehabilitation, although the employee may be reassigned to a nonsafety related position. If these procedural safeguards are not met or if the random testing is used where it is not necessary to achieve a safety purpose, then such tests should be invalidated under the Fourth Amendment.

These procedural safeguards are intended to illustrate that it is possible to reconcile conflicting values in a way that preserves individual dignity and liberty to the greatest extent possible. It is not really a question of choosing between the passenger's expectation of safe transportation or the right of the operator to personal privacy; it is the challenge of accommodating each interest in a way that does the least damage to the other.

3. Reconciling the Interests of the Child, the Parents, and the Medical Profession in Determining the Proper Treatment of Severely Handicapped Children

Advances in medical technology allow doctors to sustain the lives of handicapped infants who formerly had little chance for survival. The issue of the proper treatment of severely handicapped infants brings to bear the often conflicting interests of the child, the child's family, the doctor, the hospital and its bio-ethical committees, as well as those of government agencies and institutions.

The process of reconciliation must begin with the presumption that life is the most fundamental right enjoyed by every human being. Yet, this does not mean that life must be preserved whatever the costs, circumstances or condition of the infant patient. A zealous concern for the handicapped should not blind one to the fact that there may be medical procedures so painful or so futile that an infant's "best interests" are better served by refraining from treatment.

The federal government, fearful that the "best interests" of handicapped infants were not being sufficiently protected by either families or physicians, recently promulgated regulations establishing regulatory requirements for the treatment of such infants. These regulations stress that medical treatment decisions must be based on objective medical information rather than "subjective opinions about the future 'quality of life' of a retarded or disabled person." (*Child Abuse Neglect Prevention and Treatment Program,* "Baby Doe Regulations.") However laudable the goals of these guidelines, they threaten to do more harm than good to the interests of handicapped infants.

The "Baby Doe Regulations" pose a threat to the interests of handicapped infants because they unduly restrict the factors upon which families and medical professionals can legally base their treatment decisions. By limiting decisionmakers to "objective" medical criteria, these regulations deny the affected parties the opportunity to bring their own judgment and ethics to bear on this intensely personal decision.

In the end, if the premise of individual dignity and liberty unfettered by governmental intrusion is to have meaning, the excruciatingly painful decisions surrounding the medical care of a severely handicapped infant must be a *private* one made by the family. In making this decision, the family often will feel the need to seek counsel from the expert medical opinions of the doctors providing care for the child and/or the hospital bio-ethics committee. Government, however, does not bring to the table any necessary expertise or insight. Governmental intervention, therefore, must occur only when the primary decisionmaker (the family) has somehow abdicated its responsibilities through neglect or malfeasance. To do otherwise is to allow unwarranted, and unnecessary, intrusion into private family affairs and to substitute government-imposed values for private decisionmaking that should be protected from government interference as a valued right of individual liberty and privacy.

The central policy issues involved in so-called "Baby Doe" cases— how and when to proscribe public rules to influence or constrain private decisions about medical care—highlights the tension between public authority and private choices. The strength of the nation's health care system has been its diversity and the freedom of choice it allows. Few issues are more intensely private than matters of health and life and death. For some, non-conventional therapies have been effective, whereas government-dictated solutions, *e.g.*, the swine flu vaccinations, sometimes have not. If individual liberty and the strength of our medical system are to be preserved in the years to come, both state and federal governments must resist the temptation to become a primary player in the world of medical decisionmaking.

4. Affirmative Action and Individual Dignity

Constitutional guarantees notwithstanding, governmental decisionmaking in such areas as education, employment and housing has for nearly two centuries differentiated on the basis of a person's race or sex. The great promise of individual dignity and equal opportunity has in reality often yielded to government-imposed or sanctioned discrimination in schools, houses and jobs. For decades, minorities sought a color blind society that would not condone such distinctions. Yet during the last 30 years minorities and women increasingly have called upon government to recognize their legitimate interests as minorities and to take affirmative action to advance those interests. Having achieved a legal framework that is color blind, it has become apparent that discrimination is so firmly entrenched in the traditions and social fabric of our society that only color-conscious or sex-conscious governmental intervention can now provide the equal access the law desires.

Affirmative action programs may appear to be inconsistent with the premise of individual dignity. They substitute a kind of collectivism for unfettered individual self-advancement. Affirmative action plans attempt to redress inequalities by permitting groups that have suffered racism or sexism in the past to claim their share of the benefits otherwise achieved through individual effort. They also threaten our notion of individual rights and responsibilities which holds that legal burdens should bear some relationship to individual wrongdoing. Individuals may be denied access to benefits, in favor of others who are members of discriminated-against groups, when those burdened may bear no personal responsibility for the discrimination at issue.

It cannot be denied that the conflicts presented by affirmative action are real. Government intervention may deny a white male a position in medical school, a government contract or a job, thus depriving him of an opportunity he might otherwise have in a free society to realize his own potential. On the other hand, the vestiges of racial and sex discrimination are so deeply engrained, that laws merely banning discrimination simply scrape the surface and perpetuate the gap between the promise and the reality that has characterized the American experiment for so many of our citizens.

In the end, reconciling the conflict requires recognition of the fact that the premise of individual dignity and liberty is meaningless if it does not have significance for all Americans regardless of race, sex or national origin. For centuries, government-sanctioned discrimination has denied the full opportunities of liberty to certain members of our society. The effects of such laws have permeated every aspect of our economy and culture. In a diverse and free economic and social structure, with limited governmental powers, merely changing the laws does not eradicate centuries of tradition overnight. Affirmative action addresses these discriminatory effects and bridges the gap between the law's promise and society's performance. Affirmative action accelerates the timetable by which the opportunities of liberty will be extended to all members of our society.

In the process, some individuals will be disadvantaged. But preserving and advancing this fundamental premise of liberty is rarely without cost to individuals. In other contexts, the costs may be measured in lives lost on battlefields, in damaged reputations to public officials, or in opportunities denied children because of their parents' decisions. As Justice Powell wrote in *Wygant v. Jackson Board of Education*, "As part of this nation's dedication to eradicating racial discrimination, innocent persons may be called upon to bear some of the burden of the remedies." Liberty always has its price.

The price, of course, must be reasonable. To minimize the burdens placed on individuals, affirmative action programs must be based on a finding of past statutory or constitutional violation or clear evidence of a "manifest imbalance in traditionally segregated job categories." See *Johnson v. Santa Clara County*. That is, programs which create preferences for women and minorities must genuinely serve a remedial purpose. The more closely an affirmative action plan adheres to a remedial purpose, the less likely it will infringe unreasonably on the interests of "innocent" third parties. And the remedies can be tailored to minimize the harm to third parties. Denial of a possible future job opportunity is less burdensome than the loss of an existing job. Remedies should be designed to foster access to the economic and social structure; advancement within that structure should be based solely on merit.

Affirmative action specifically tailored to ferret out the vestiges of government-sanctioned discrimination is a necessary tool in the continuing struggle to realize the American promise of individual dignity and liberty. Sustaining and building upon the progress of the past thirty years will require the resourceful and constrained use of such tools as competing interests are accommodated, conflicting rights reconciled, and age-old principles applied to an increasingly complex and challenging current context.

The Changing American Family

Representative Nancy Johnson

In the 1980s, America rediscovered the family.

Families have always been with us, but never has there been so broad a consensus that the interests of families must be recognized in the formulation of national policy as that which has emerged during the Reagan years.

At the root of the new movement is the recognition that families are important. In an early State of the Union address, President Reagan said:

> "[O]ur most precious resources, our greatest hope for the future, are the minds and hearts of our people, especially our children. We can help them build tomorrow by strengthening our community of shared values . . . faith, work, family, neighborhood, freedom, and peace are not just words. They are expressions of what America means; definitions of what makes us a good and loving people."

President Reagan was not hearkening back to a simpler time in the distant past; he was setting priorities for the present. Families today are under great stress. Adolescent pregnancy and an exponential rise in the rate of divorce are dramatic examples of the underlying social pressures. If we are to successfully develop policies to address the new and challenging circumstances of America's families, we must find new ways to couple private and public strengths and resources.

We must rethink many government policies and honestly recognize the importance of individual values to their success. As we have learned to use public policy to leverage economic development, so we must use public policy to assure the growth of strong families and sound values.

Former Secretary of Labor Bill Brock has observed that "the future belongs to those who hear it coming." Government is just beginning to hear its families.

Tax reform legislation passed in 1986 eased the tax burden on low income families and single heads-of-households, and while repealing dozens of tax credits, preserved the individual tax credit for low income families.

Welfare reform was catapulted to the top of the social agenda by President Reagan—and then the Congress—because they recognized that the present welfare system is hurting, not helping, families.

The remarkable response to the Department of Education's study, "A Nation at Risk," reflected the public perception that education was failing our children and families.

We do not need another task force, however, to help families. We need to attack problems facing families with early intervention and prevention strategies. We do not need more rhetoric about the importance of families without responsible plans to translate talk into action. Poor families, working families, families with children and with elderly parents cry out for honest, realistic answers; in short, pro-family policies.

An effective family policy must address many new issues and reform many existing programs and policies. The following pages discuss some of the essentials of a progressive, Republican family policy, and the direction I believe that the GOP should take if it is to build on the good record of its past accomplishments and provide leadership for the future.

HELPING WORKING FAMILIES

The working mother today is the rule rather than the exception. Of the approximately 52 million American children under age 15, more than 29 million have mothers who work. Nineteen million of these same children have mothers who work full-time. Consequently, any policy affecting families must reflect an understanding of the new relationship between families and the workforce. Not only in single-parent families, but in two-parent families as well, parents share breadwinning and parenting duties.

According to the Congressional Budget Office, in 1985 two-thirds of women with children under 18 were in the paid labor force. A slightly smaller percentage—about 60 percent—had children under six. In contrast, following World War II only 26 percent of married women with children between the ages of 6 and 17 worked. Today, the "traditional" two-parent, one breadwinner family comprises less than ten percent of all families.

As a result, today's government policies must recognize the dependence of our economy on a workforce of employees with serious family responsibilities. Among the pro-family policies that must be championed by Republicans to address the needs of this new workforce are family leave, child care, flexible work hours and "cafeteria" benefit plans. Employees must be allowed to choose from benefits that will address their needs and those of their families.

Child care services have not evolved to meet the needs of working families. We face an epidemic of latchkey kids—school-age children who supervise themselves after school until their parents return from work—and a great shortage of affordable, good care for pre-schoolers. In particular, low income parents consistently report that the lack of affordable child care is the single greatest barrier to becoming and staying employed.

And child care is expensive. Generally only food, rent and taxes command a greater share of the family budget. Yet, federal programs help only those whose means are so limited that they qualify for welfare or help under Title XX of the Social Services Block Grant, or whose incomes are high enough to afford the full cost of day care but benefit from an off-setting tax credit at the end of the year. The result is, working poor families, struggling at or just above poverty, are practically untouched by federal child care assistance programs.

Consequently, we must first broadly reform federal child care policy to make subsidies serve all equitably. But we must address the issue of the quality of the care available for our children as well.

Legislation I proposed in the 99th Congress embodies this needed, broad commitment to increase access, improve quality and assure affordability of day care. The program would set up a system of child care certificates which would provide income-related subsidies to families to enable them to buy day care at licensed day care centers, or registered or licensed family day care homes. Just like our current Dependent Care Tax Credit, these new subsidies must preserve parents' rights within broad parameters to choose the care setting that is best for their child.

The legislation would also encourage the development of a new professionalism among family day care home providers. It would better assist parents in overseeing their child's care environment, and so enhance the quality of child care. It would require states to upgrade their licensing and certification systems to improve the quality of care, and would set up outreach programs to providers and parents to provide training to the former, instruction in oversight to the latter, and technical assistance and support to both.

Beyond adopting public policies to increase the availability, affordability, and quality of child care, we must assure that employees can leave work to care for critically-ill children and encourage the kind of flexible work hours that enable parents to minimize out-of-home care. As the work place has been required to respond to safety and environmental concerns, so it must now respond to family concerns and recognize its dependence on people with significant parenting and elder care responsibilities.

Finally, and no less important than the issues of quality, equity, and flexibility for out-of-home care, is the need to provide a tax credit to those families in which one parent stays home to care for the children. This kind of economic support for parents of young children is justified and will shelter young families from some of the economic pressures that force both parents to seek work. It gives young families a fighting chance at financial stability and is cost effective for society.

FAMILIES IN NEED

To paraphrase Ralph Waldo Emerson, the true test of a civilization is how it treats its poor. Government is not now supporting families in meeting their basic needs nor assuring them the opportunity that is the great promise of democracy.

The shape of the family in America has changed and sound pro-family policies must reflect the ramifications of that fact. Fewer than seven percent of intact, married-couple families have incomes below the poverty line [The New Consensus on Family and Welfare]. But more than 34 percent of families headed by a woman are poor, and the percentage of poor female-headed households is increasing rapidly. In fact, children in female-headed households constitute the largest poverty group.

Republicans must renew efforts to identify and augment programs that address poverty, help families stay together, nurture the development of the nation's disadvantaged children, and assist families in neutralizing the fallout of rapid social change. We need to reassess our philosophical opposition to such programs as public assistance to two-parent families like the Aid to Families with Dependent Children Unemployed Parent Program. Statistics in more than one state have shown that when this two-parent stipend is discontinued for families, marriages break up so the children will remain eligible for assistance. We must support the expansion of proven programs like Head Start and the Supplemental Food Program for Women, Infants and Children (WIC), complementing them with a welfare system that fosters the development of personal responsibility. We must knit these policies together with new approaches to drug dependence, housing problems, unemployment and divorce that contribute to the family breakdowns that devastate lives.

Aid to Families with Dependent Children (AFDC), the program we usually think of as welfare, was originally conceived during the Great Depression as a stipend for widows and orphans. Even in an era when the majority of mothers are working, AFDC still treats low-income adults like the dependent widows and orphans of 50 years ago.

A Republican president, Ronald Reagan, forced welfare reform to the top of the national agenda. Republicans in Congress are pressing hard for reforms that strengthen families by fostering the development of recipients' parenting and job skills—before families become trapped on welfare—while assuring health care benefits and day care for children.

Early intervention is especially important for teen mothers. A woman who has her first child as a teenager is at great risk of entrapment on welfare for ten years or more. Of all women under 30 who are receiving AFDC, as many as 71 percent had their first child as a teenager. Only half of the girls who gave birth before they were 18 are likely to finish school.

Statistics confirm that the relationship between welfare dependence and teenage pregnancy is a strong one. Common sense tells us that any program that would allow a young parent who has dropped out of high school to say no to education, job training or parenting classes is not helping that individual—or the children. Yet the present program allows a welfare recipient to stay home, isolated and out of a developmentally challenging environment, until her youngest child is six. This fosters dependence, not independence.

The problems of fathers, too, must be addressed if we are to have a sound national pro-family policy. In perpetuating the idea that family responsibilities are women's work, as our present welfare system does, we send a clear message to young men that fatherhood and their contribution to the well-being of their families is not significant to society. Sound policy should address the situation of unemployed, unmarried fathers by requiring the same participation in education, training and work programs of non-supporting fathers that we do of welfare-dependent women.

Welfare is far too expensive, both in terms of the cost of entrapping women and children in poverty and in terms of wasting human capital in a nation with a shrinking labor pool, growing economy and competitive international market. The AFDC program needs to be refocused. At the root of welfare reform is getting people back to work—for their own sake and for the sake of the economy.

Likewise, the "K—12" concept of education does not prevent educational problems that could be solved before a child enrolls in school. If we care about strong families, we should direct preventive developmental services at the children who now arrive at kindergarten with educational deficits. Programs such as "Even Start," proposed by Republican Representative Bill Goodling, reaches out to address young children's educational problems in their homes, and simultaneously addresses family educational problems such as language problems. This holistic, preventive approach serves to better prepare a child for school and aligns education with building stronger families who can have greater economic opportunity.

Access to affordable housing is another basic family need, the shortage of which is precipitating family breakup. Once the American dream, housing is fast becoming a national nightmare. According to the U.S. Conference of Mayors, in the present decade homelessness is growing at an annual rate of nearly 25 percent.

It is frightening that as many as one-third of the new homeless are families with children. Surprisingly, one-fifth of the homeless are working. Even middle-class families are being pressured by housing prices. While real family income did not increase between 1973 and 1984, Federal National Mortgage Association Chairman David O. Maxwell noted that during the same 11-year span, "housing prices rose so swiftly that the median-priced house came to absorb more than twice as much of the median family income."

The crisis in housing for families is rapidly escalating. The number of substandard units grows and thousands of federal contracts for low-income housing units are expiring. It is tragically easy to document the failure of policy makers to anticipate today's housing problems and develop initiatives to replace programs like Section 8 subsidies, which, while very expensive, succeeded in providing decent housing to poor families.

In the long-term, the solution is not additional funds to emergency shelter programs or new construction subsidies guaranteeing developer profits. Rather, as with most challlenges, long-term strategies have the best chance of success when responsibility is shared by all levels of government *and* the private sector as well as the private family beneficiary.

Local administrators, state agencies and the federal government can work as partners with the private sector in the creation of affordable housing. Isolated community-based organizations across the country are already revitalizing the "American Dream" through "sweat-equity" projects which benefit thousands of low-income families. Building on successful, innovative programs, federal low-interest loans could provide the seed money to enable local neighborhood housing organizations to oversee the purchase of substandard housing, using in part tenant "sweat equity" to reduce the cost of renovation and providing the training in tenant governance so important to the success of cooperatives or condominium associations.

Federal dollars could be linked with state and local contributions to establish revolving loan funds, which could offer low-income loans to construct or purchase affordable housing units. In recognition of past policy failures, low-income owners would be required upon the sale of their homes to return to the revolving fund a percentage of the sale equivalent to the percentage of public subsidy in the original purchase. This strategy would assure that low-income subsidies would retain their original buying power over time without regard to shifts in the market.

Decent housing is essential to stable families; so is affordable health care. American medical advances have produced one of the healthiest populations in the world and one with a low mortality rate. But, a significant minority of Americans do not have access to routine medical attention because they cannot afford health insurance.

In 1985 employer plans covered 132 million people. The Medicaid program protects families dependent on welfare and Medicare alleviates some of the burden on our senior citizens. But significant holes in our health care delivery system need to be addressed.

Approximately 35 million people are medically indigent. Many of these people are workers with families who work for small businesses without health care benefits. Others are displaced workers who are too old to be easily employed, not affluent enough to afford coverage, and too young to qualify for Medicare.

The Medicare program covers the cost of hospitalization for acute illness, but many people of advanced age are in greater need of prescription and in-home assistance, for which Medicare reimbursement is very limited. Assistance with the high cost of long-term nursing home care is not available at all through Medicare, and only on a very limited and nascent basis through private insurance plans. Couples are often forced to relinquish the savings of a lifetime in order to meet the income standards for nursing home care assistance under Medicaid.

These are conditions that concern all of us. Health care is everyone's need, and the burden for providing it must be shared by all, access to needed care must be guaranteed by all.

Republicans have put forth a number of promising proposals. The 1987 debate on medicare coverage for catastrophic health care expenses engendered a creative long-term care proposal from the Republican side, encouraging individual initiative by allowing tax exempt investments. Other ad-hoc groups of Republicans are developing proposals to make the Medicaid program available to the presently uninsured through variable copayments. We, as a party, need to fully develop ideas to meet the growing need for health care insurance among those now not covered and to more comprehensively meet the needs of low-income children and of the elderly.

CONCLUSION

Helping families become and remain strong and independent should be a primary goal in the development of our domestic policies. We must marshal the resources of all levels of government and more rationally link public and private capabilities to achieve this goal.

Successful policies of the future will address family issues holistically and preventively. Family leave, child care, flexible work hours and broader benefit plans are some of the workplace issues of the day, much as occupational safety and environmental concerns were the workplace issues of the 1970s. Early intervention can address growing educational deficits and prevent family problems of interpersonal and substance from becoming costly societal problems. Health care and housing must be available and affordable, and more realistic policies must reduce long-term welfare dependence.

The Republican Party has long understood the central importance of families and sound values to our success as a nation, and equally important, the necessity for shared responsibility if government and its citizens are to succeed in solving pressing problems. Our party's track record in creating a vital partnership between the public and private sector has been outstanding. We must now assure this approach addresses the very human challenges that face the American family in the closing decades of the twentieth century.

"Strong families benefit the entire society . . . . raising children is not a series of private concerns, but one in which we all have a vested interest," David Blankenhorn, director of the Institute for American Values, has observed. It is entirely appropriate that government rise to the challenge of supporting the growth of strong families in our fast-paced, changing world.

Education and Training in the Public Debate

William C. Clohan, Jr.

The Republican or Democratic candidate who wins the 1988 presidential election will probably be the one who best communicates a clear and substantive direction in federal education and training policy. That is not to say that education will be the one, or most important, issue on the national agenda and in the national debate. However, as was observed in a recent *Wall Street Journal* article, education will be a major issue in presidential politics for the first time in perhaps 25 years.

In the Fall of 1987, Republican candidates took the lead in seizing education as an important concept and proposed a number of possibilities for education reform at the federal level. Historically, Republicans have allowed Democrats to seize the initiative in the education debate. Moreover, Democrats have generally been advocates for a stronger federal role, more federal spending, and have had a stronger alignment with the teachers' union.

This chapter explores the changing society as we know it in the United States, relates the American experience in dealing with the educational and training needs for that change, identifies some of the lessons learned as a result of the federal government's experiment with different educational programs and then discusses the current reforms that are being debated at the federal and state level. Without such an approach to education and training policy many candidates may find themselves at odds with themselves during debates and make inconsistent policy recommendations. In many ways, the context of the education and training debate is as important at the national level as the actual specific recommendations. This was borne out in the 1980 presidential election, during which Candidate Ronald Reagan argued strongly for a decreased federal role in education.

THE CONTEXT OF THE DEBATE

During the Reagan administration, there has been a plethora of reports on statistical trends in education and training which have led to the following general conclusions:

• Basic skills and functional literacy are sorely lacking in American society.
• A serious labor shortage is emerging for skilled blue collar craftsmen and has increased concern that the United States cannot respond quickly to an international crisis.
• Students in the nation's public schools lack important literary and historical knowledge due to an emphasis on skills over knowledge.
• Graduate science training for U.S. citizens is falling behind America's demand and the U.S. must depend on foreign scientists to meet the needs of today's technological society.
• Labor supply and demand will be in imbalance.
• Jobs will move from goods-producing industries to an information, communications industry.
• Many new and existing jobs will require higher levels of analytical and communications skills.
• Level of literacy required will continue to rise beyond mere reading and writing ability.

At first glance, the needs described above and the possible solutions to those problems are somewhat contradictory. How can we focus on job skills when basic literacy skills are so deficient? Is there enough room in a high school or college curriculum to teach the classics and foreign languages if more specific job training is necessary to prepare a student for a job? Won't the overemphasis on science and engineering at the post-graduate level serve only to reduce the source of our cultural tradition through the humanities and the arts? All of the above problems must be solved and governmental, as well as private, resources must be dedicated to those solutions.

Trade "competitiveness" has been one of the buzzwords of the 100th Congress. Almost every major issue affecting our economy has been dealt with by proposing programs to make the United States more "competitive" in the international marketplace. Education and training legislation has not only escaped the penumbra of "competitiveness," it has resulted in substantial proposals to make the U.S. more competitive. The following pages discuss the facts behind the education and training problems.

THE AMERICAN EDUCATIONAL EXPERIENCE

In the same year as the United States gained its independence 211 years ago, Adam Smith wrote in *The Wealth of Nations:*

> "The wealth of a nation was very much determined by the quality of its workforce. Human resources provide the basis of productivity and productivity growth. Through individual workers and managers come creativity and innovation, experience and expertise and production in sales. Without a literate, skilled, healthy, and motivated workforce, capital or technology cannot create a productive environment."

A healthy educational system is essential for any nation, developed or developing, to meet the new demands of an ever-changing society. The traditionalists in the United States have always advocated a broad general liberal arts education. This form of education has been the foundation for a well-educated society which has the capacity to respond to the changing needs and problems of the society. Since World War II there has been the realization that formal, job-specific skills training is also necessary in order for a society, its economy, businesses and industry, to be productive.

The educational system of the United States is not really a "system." In fact, it is quite diverse and decentralized. At the elementary and secondary levels, the public school system is generally run by the individual states and localities and provides the primary education for most of our children. Historically, parochial or church-related schools have provided a small, but consistent portion of the education of our children. In particular, Catholic-related schools have served the needs of many inner-city youth.

In recent years, an explosion of Protestant fundamentalist church-related schools have burgeoned throughout the United States. In large part, this tremendous growth was due to the feeling on the part of parents and churches that the public school education was "Godless" and did not teach the moral principles which fundamentally underpin American society. Moreover, many religious fundamentalists believe that the discussion of secular humanism and social Darwinism was warping the minds of children and leading to a reduction in educational quality and test scores, social and sexual promiscuity, and elimination of values.

At the postsecondary or higher education level, the educational system is even more diverse. Public universities and colleges, private baccalaureate and graduate institutions, two-year public community colleges, private short-term training institutions, and public vocational institutions constitute a myriad of education providers which, in fact, have served well the postsecondary needs of America.

The role of the federal government in this educational system in the United States is quite limited. For example, less than seven percent of all funding for elementary and secondary education is provided by the federal government and only approximately 50 percent of postsecondary funding comes from Washington. In large part, this results from the interpretation of the Constitution that education is a function which is reserved for the states. While this interpretation is more historical than constitutional, the role of the federal government has been very limited until the last 20 years.

After World War II, returning military veterans received grants and loans under the "GI Bill." This financial support greatly expanded access to postsecondary education and invigorated American society with a more knowledgeable workforce. In the mid-1960s, President Johnson's "Great Society" programs tremendously expanded the involvement of the central government in elementary, secondary, vocational and postsecondary education. A system of loans and work-study programs was authorized by the Higher Education Act of 1965; in 1972 grants were included. A major program for disadvantaged elementary and secondary students was authorized by the Elementary and Secondary Education Act of 1965. A "free and appropriate education" was guaranteed to all handicapped young people in 1973.

With these new laws came not only substantial federal funding, but also federal requirements and intervention in day-to-day decision-making. Although states and localities provided the greatest share of funds for education, national policy was driven by the requirements in federal law.

The Great Society also spawned the Job Corps program and increased funding for training and vocational education. In 1973, the nation's many overlapping manpower programs were merged into the Comprehensive and Employment Training Act (CETA). Approximately one-third of CETA's initial funding was for training-related programs. The remainder went toward public service employment and summer jobs for youth. One of the objectives of CETA was to decentralize federal authority by delegating the responsibility of administering training programs to state and local governments. The state and local authorities were free to develop a broad range of employment programs to match their community's needs.

The CETA program has since been replaced by the Job Training Partnership Act (JTPA), an effort to broaden the role of businesses in establishing national and local training priorities. Also, public employment jobs have been all but eliminated and increased funding is targeted to actual job training.

Since 1981, the Reagan administration has taken a more decentralized perspective on education at all levels and tried to overturn much of the federal role in education initiated between 1965 and 1980. President Reagan, until recently, has proposed the elimination of the Department of Education, which was established in 1978. The U.S. Congress has ignored this effort almost totally, perhaps symbolically to demonstrate the necessity for an emphasis on education to meet the demands of a technologically-based society. President Reagan has further unsuccessfully sought to reduce funding across-the-board for education and has successfully stimulated the use of volunteers in the private sector to promote educational excellence.

The publication of a study entitled "A Nation at Risk," produced by the Secretary of Education in 1983, has either led to major educational reforms throughout the country or mirrors reform that it had already begun prior to 1983. Study after study since then has identified problems with the U.S. public education system. Some of those problems are a result of the educational system itself, but many result from the ills of society which invariably affect school children. The following statistics and factors evidence problems which face educators and policymakers in the coming decades:

• The number of youth entering the workforce will decrease as a percentage of youth workforce increases.

• The number of high school dropouts will increase, rising above the one million children who now drop out of school each year.

• Youth unemployment is expected to increase.

• Twenty-three million adults are today considered functionally illiterate and these numbers are expected to worsen.

• Teenage pregnancy will become more common than ever.

• The incidence of female head of households will continue to increase.

• Women will account for two-thirds of the labor force growth during the 1980s and 1990s.

• Two working-parent families will become more common, increasing the demand for child care.

• Prime age workers (25–54 years of age) will account for about 75 percent of the 1995 workforce.

• The prospects for permanent dislocation of workers are expected to increase.

• The population aged 55 and over will increase.

• Workers with critical technical skills will be retiring at an increasingly rapid rate.

• Illegal immigration will be an increasingly significant factor in the competition for entry-level jobs.

• Immigrants will represent the largest share of the increase in the population since World War II.

THE CHANGING WORKPLACE

Since 1945, the developed nations have enjoyed unusual prosperity and economic growth. Although at times we feel frustrated with the economies of each of our respective countries, in general we are much better off than we were prior to 1940. The question facing us is whether our countries can maintain that growth, given the complex technological changes and the economic uncertainty confronting us.

The computer, in particular, has revolutionized our societies and we both fear it and acknowledge it as a force with which to reckon. How we use technology in the coming decades will determine how much we produce and how high our standard of living will be. Technology is a product of an education system which fosters growth, experimentation and proper use of natural and human resources.

There is no doubt that the commercial or professional type computers being used by industry will revolutionize industry. Robotics and sophisticated mainframe computers will do much of the "thinking" and "working" that is normally done by humans in the day-to-day work environment. Perhaps as great a revolution is the less expensive and relatively simple microcomputer which is, at least in the United States, available to and used by a significant portion of the population. Where just five years ago a personal microcomputer was an anamoly, today it is appreciated as a technological tool almost as necessary as a telephone or automobile.

The expanding use of computers will undoubtedly lead to decentralization of jobs through contracting out or working at home. On the other hand, some functions will become more centralized because of the ability of the masses to tie into a central computer system. There are almost 150 occupations in the U.S. in which workers now use computers. However, only one-third of the workforce was employed in these occupations and less than half of these workers were using computers. Most of the computer users do not require major long-term training or require the ability to write computer programs. Over 85 percent operate equipment with standardized software for data or word processing, information storage/retrieval or industrial process control.

The computer skills needed in most occupations are only a small part of the total work skills needed. Basic academic skills, occupational knowledge, problem-solving and interpersonal skills will be the most important ingredients for success in the workplace. Thus, education will be increasingly important for success. Functionally illiterate adults are likely to have the most difficulty in the labor market.

The nature of the workplace is not only affected by increased technology. In some ways, increased technology is both the cause and the effect of the change in the types of jobs that will be available in the coming decades. In the past ten years, of the 20 million new jobs created in the United States, only five percent were in manufacturing while 90 percent were in the service and information industries. By the end of the century, an estimated five to 15 million manufacturing jobs will be restructured. Nine out of 10 of the new jobs developed between 1984 and 1995 will be in the service sector. These jobs will not necessarily be "high tech" but will require higher levels of skills.

By 1990, an estimated three out of four American jobs will require some education or technical training beyond high school. These new jobs will not occur at major manufacturing companies, but at smaller companies where employers often lack the resources for formal training programs. While small businesses can be expected to account for the majority of new jobs, it is particularly difficult for them to be established in predominantly depressed or center-city areas because they lack capital investment from commercial banks. Employers already spend an estimated $30 billion on formal job training and retraining in the United States. One in every eight working Americans receives at least one formal training course each year.

For most of our history, Americans have been in love with change or newness. Early in the nineteeth century, a Frenchman we love to quote, Alexis de Tocqueville, described in *Democracy in America* a chance encounter with an American sailor who explained to the bemused Frenchman why it was unnecessary in America to build sailing ships sturdy enough to last for decades. Progress in the art of shipbuilding is so swift and certain, the sailor said, that any ship, after only a brief time on the seas, is sure to be replaced by a newer, better vessel.

Change and progress have been marked traits of Americans throughout history, but our confidence has been shaken over the past two decades. In the 1970s, productivity has risen much faster in countries such as France, West Germany and Japan. How the United States deals with these problems will determine how successful our economy will be in the coming years. Obviously, closer self-scrutiny is necessary.

THE LESSONS LEARNED AND CURRENT REFORMS

The Great Society programs spawned during the mid-1960s have been somewhat successful but not spectacularly so. Large amounts of federal dollars have been spent on programs which have resulted in an increase of access to both elementary, secondary and postsecondary education, particularly among minorities and students from low-income families. These programs have engendered a great debate about the impact the lessening of entrance requirements has on the quality of education, particularly at the postsecondary level.

"Educational excellence" is the guiding light of the current administration in Washington. That excellence is fostered, says President Reagan, by choice among types of education providers. To encourage the choice, the Reagan administration has proposed that Congress enact laws which provide tuition tax credits for parents of students attending non-public elementary and secondary institutions. Furthermore, the administration has proposed that some form of educational voucher be available to public school students so that they may choose to go to other types of public schools or private schools where their needs can be better met.

The debate, precipitated by a discussion of tuition tax credits and educational vouchers, particularly when it is merged with the debate over prayer in schools and other church/state issues, is a very controversial one. Although major education reforms have taken place in the past five years in more than 30 of the 50 states of the country, few states have implemented any programs similar to tuition tax credits or educational vouchers. One reason for this is that the American public has a preoccupation with limiting state involvement in church or church-related activities.

Twenty years ago "access" to education was the prime focus of federal legislation. The establishment and expansion of new federal programs was to solve the access problem. In the ensuing decades, "quality" was given less attention. In recent months, the issue of quality has come to the fore in the national educational debate. Education Secretary William Bennett has espoused accountability in higher education and competitiveness between public and private elementary/secondary institutions to ensure quality. Recent regulations proposed by the secretary would require all accrediting bodies to measure "outcomes" of the educational process. Although the measurement would be primarily left to the education institutions, the proposed process would move away from the traditional accreditation method of evaluating imputs, such as pupil/teacher ratios and number of volumes in the library.

Another administration reform has been the initiation of block grants to states and localities to carry out educational functions. While the Great Society programs created very specific requirements for the expenditure of federal dollars, the education laws enacted in the past four years have provided a great deal of flexibility to states and localities determining educational priorities and mechanisms for implementing those priorities.

The myriad of grant, loan and work-study assistance available at the postsecondary level has historically been in a voucher form. That is to say, students are determined to be eligible for the aid and then they can "shop" with that federal aid at various colleges and universities throughout the country. Thus, the federal higher education program assistance provides both access and choice to all types of students. In fact, it can be argued that any person with the requisite academic ability can find the financial capability to go to college or enter some form of postsecondary vocational program.

Perhaps the best example of how major reform can significantly alter the conduct of manpower training and significantly increase the benefit using fewer federal dollars is the preliminary success of the Job Training Partnership Act (JTPA). As noted earlier, it replaced a rather cumbersome and untargeted program entitled the Comprehensive Employment and Training Act (CETA). Under the JTPA, business is involved to a large extent in deciding where federal dollars will be spent and on what type of training. More than 50 percent of the national advisory board under JTPA is to be drawn from the business community. State and local advisory committees also must be composed of a majority of business people. The remaining members of the advisory committee are local policymakers, educators and representatives of labor.

Another reform within JTPA has been the requirement that many of the funds be allocated based on the performance of the educational provider. Previously, grants were made to educational institutions and other training entities and no successful completion or employment success was expected. Now, many JTPA recipients only receive funds if the trainees successfully complete their coursework and find jobs. This performance-based focus has resulted in higher placement rates and a better cost-benefit to the federal government. It is likely to be replicated in some form in other federal education and training laws in the coming years.

Dispersed decisionmaking, whether at the universities or in the elementary and secondary schools, will not work well unless there are sufficient incentives to do a good job. Matching funds from private sources, performance-based contracting, incentive payments for successful completion of objectives, or disincentives when the objective is not met will lead to higher productivity within the educational system. While this may sound contrary to the traditional liberal arts tradition where "productivity" is not necessarily an objective, we need to realize that in a technologically-based society training and retraining will occur almost every five years. We cannot afford to ignore skills training because of our inherent desire to provide education in the classics.

Further, broad-based literacy and skills training is essential for a society to run successfully. In the United States, skills training is no longer provided through an apprenticeship system. Over half of the retraining which occurs comes from industry-supported or in-house education. Over 75 percent of the remainder is provided by private profitmaking education institutions. Nations need to be responsive to the need for continual upgrading of their educational system and the use of alternative means of education and training.

GENERAL POLICY POSITIONS

The environment discussed above, in which today's education and training debate will occur, forces policymakers to focus on general policy principles before specific programmatic changes can be suggested. This section discusses some principles which can serve as the basis for new education policy.

Education is a Shared Responsibility Between Parents, Localities, States and the Federal Government

Education is not now, nor should it be, primarily a federal function. However, the federal government does have responsibility for certain facets of education in the United States. There are national concerns, national problems and, ultimately, national solutions. We must not be blinded by our aversion to ideas which may include the involvement of the federal government.

The shared responsibility between parents, localities, states and the federal government should be a creative partnership. This partnership should be flexible and must include the strengths of each of the partners. Our nation's founding fathers never contemplated the direct involvement of the federal government in the education of the nation's children; therefore, the responsibility for that education originally was a function of the parent and the church. With few exceptions, the involvement of localities and states came later. The establishment of a public system of elementary and secondary education coincided with the industrialization of our society. During the nineteenth century, the passage of the Morrill Act, which established land-grant universities and a national Department of Education, indicated that the federal government was eventually to be involved.

During the past twenty years, the federal government has taken a leadership role in establishing programs which sought to deal with the educational problems of our society. The shared responsibility and partnership is richer because of those programs.

The Federal Government Should Play a Leadership Role in Education

Fear of intrusion by the federal government in local education policymaking has led some Republicans to reject totally the involvement of the federal government in the educational process. This, in large part, explains the rejection by some of a cabinet-level Department of Education. The 1980 GOP platform and the efforts of the administration during the past several years have been to reorganize the Department into an independent agency, to place the federal programs in a multitude of other departments, or to place the Department as a sub-unit of an existing department. Much time and energy was spent on this political objective, all to no avail.

Preoccupation with the organizational structure used to administer federal programs is counterproductive. Whether the federal education programs exist in a cabinet-level agency is not the ultimate criteria by which the federal role should be judged. While the Department is a symbol of federal interest in education, ultimately the substance of the federal programs are the most important feature of the federal role. Focus should be placed on those programs to make them more successful and less intrusive.

The next administration should set the national tone for educational reform. This does not mean a federal regulatory or activists' involvement in state and local decision-making. However, it does require supportive actions and constructively critical comments regarding the nature of education in the United States.

The Department of Education has served and should continue to serve as a visible pulpit from which an administration can stimulate a national awareness of the importance of education. The report of the President's Commission on Excellence in Education is the best example of the positive activities which can come from high visibility within the federal Executive Branch. Similar studies and open forums should continue.

Education Must Carefully Balance the Laudable Goals of Excellence,
Equity and Experimentation

The focus on educational excellence as the result of the report "A Nation at Risk" bears with it a significant risk. The equally important concept of equity must not be diminished in the effort to create excellence.

There were some failures in the federal programs established during the past twenty years, but, on balance, they have raised our societal and educational awareness to new heights of fairness and educational opportunity. It is not enough to blame lower test scores on those federal programs; the problems of society as a whole are much more to blame. Likewise, the criticism that lower educational achievement resulted from new methods of teaching is too simplistic.

Excellence in education is unacceptable unless all individuals, including the disadvantaged, have access to that excellent educational system. All the funding in the world is worthless without access for all to programs supported by that funding, and, likewise, equal educational opportunity is hollow without the financial support to provide the teachers, equipment, books and classrooms for that training.

A total focus on basic skills or the three R's is not the panacea for high achievement or educational excellence. While these basic educational skills provide the foundation for further study, our society must always be open to new methods of teaching and learning to prepare individuals to succeed in an ever-changing, complex society. The fact that old methods of teaching worked decades ago does not mean that they will continue to work in the future, any more than the abacus is an adequate substitute for the computer. Support from the federal government for research on new methods is essential.

Education Should Have a High Priority in the Federal Budget

Education is an investment in society's future which has a higher long-term economic return than almost any other public expenditure. To fail to provide adequate financial support for education is to mortgage the future of our country.

While the federal government has historically provided less than ten percent of the financial support for education in this country, that support is critical, on the margin, to provide for special needs populations.

It is politically naive and pragmatically unacceptable to advocate major education budget cuts. Notwithstanding the deep budget cuts in education proposed by the administration during the past several years, neither Congress nor the majority of the electorate supported such a proposal. Education is fundamental to a free society and the voters know it. To advocate a lessening of federal support for education is to impart political hari-kari.

Special Populations Require Additional Support to Ensure Equal Educational Opportunity

Disadvantaged individuals, such as the handicapped, low income students, women, and racial and linguistic minorities, require special support in order to have a real equal opportunity to succeed. The federal programs of the past twenty years have provided much of that support.

The Chapter I (formerly Title I) program has had a demonstrably positive effect on the education of low-income students. Prior to the enactment of the Education of the Handicapped Act in 1973, handicapped individuals had little access to our educational system. The broad-based federal student financial assistance programs have opened up opportunities to individuals of all backgrounds to obtain a higher education. One only has to look at the involvement and successes of female athletes in recent years to see that Title IX has provided the necessary stimulus to guarantee opportunities for women and girls in education and athletics.

The thrust for educational excellence should not result in an overemphasis on programs supporting the gifted, the talented and the high achiever. It is not enough that those high achievers remain above sea level while the less fortunate drown in mediocrity. Education policy must increase the level of the sea so that all students and individuals in our society are raised to new heights of excellence.

On the other hand, educational institutions and systems cannot and should not be the caretakers of our society. To blame societal ills on them is to ignore the problems which exist in homes, churches and communities at large.

Teachers should be considered to be *in loco parentis* for education alone and not to solve fully the discipline, drug and immorality problems which pervade our society. For too long we have expected too much from our teachers without providing enough incentive for them to be productive, let alone to excel. Merit pay and master teachers are good ideas. However, such concepts should only be put into practice when adequate basic financial support is provided for the teaching profession. To do otherwise is to make teaching an unattractive career field and the "best and brightest" will be drawn to other, more lucrative occupations.

The Federal Government Must Make Significant Investments in Science, Engineering, Mathematics and Languages in Order to Survive and Compete With Other Nations in A Rapidly Changing Technological World

The response to the Russian Sputnik was a national one. The United States saw that, as a nation, it was falling behind the rest of the world in its ability to be at the forefront of new technology. The national response included federal legislation and increased federal funding.

New problems and new technologies impel the federal government to continue that response. The challenges of trade competitiveness, space, national defense, health and international diplomacy demand that adequate federal support be provided in the years ahead. To do otherwise is to diminish the legacy we should provide for our children and our children's children.

The Federal Government Must Carefully Balance Its Desire for National Educational Diversity With Its Support for an Open System of Public Education

The public education system is one of our nation's greatest resources and should be nurtured, without unwarranted intrusion, by the federal government. If parental involvement and financial support in our public education system ever declines significantly, only the financially well-to-do could afford an excellent education.

The concept that competition will lead to excellence in education is yet unproven. If the competition involves parties in uneven bargaining positions or if one of the competitors must carry a heavier load, it may result in the demise of that party. Our public school system has carried the load for decades of educating the poor, the handicapped and the disadvantaged. That burden is an expensive one and must be paid for in some way. Therefore, any consideration of major tuition tax credit or educational voucher legislation must be coupled with an objective evaluation of its impact on the public school system.

On the other hand, the federal government must not impede the meritorious aim of providing diversity in our educational system, particularly at the postsecondary level. Our society needs to recognize that a liberal arts degree does not guarantee a job or career success; nor does a vocational education guarantee a productive society. Different individuals have different needs and different types of educational institutions are better suited to satisfy those needs. Likewise, the federal government must not impede the desires of parents to ensure that their sons and daughters receive an education at an institution which promotes moral principles consistent with their own.

Educational Institutions or Persons Who Discriminate Should Not Receive Federal Program or Tax Benefits

The Republican Party must never take the position that any form of discrimination against constitutionally-protected classes of individuals can be supported by federal program funds or tax benefits. Educational institutions or individuals who receive federal benefits should realize that with those benefits comes the concomitant responsibility to abide by the laws which provide for those benefits.

Freedom of Thought Is the Bedrock of Our Educational System, Just as Freedom of Religion Is the Foundation of Our Moral Development

Preoccupation with such legitimate issues as government-protected versus personal prayer in school, secular humanism versus moral legalism, and evolution versus creationism will not solve our nation's educational problems. As a matter of fact, these debates at the national level often tend to obfuscate "real" educational issues.

It is critical that in our free society we must never try to impose our personal beliefs on adolescents through the educational system. To state or imply that a person's value system is wrong because it is different than the beliefs of the majority of the population is to undermine the very constitutional guarantee which allows a public discussion of those rights in the first place. Though essential in a democratic society, ethical or values training must be taught with care.

The United States is a multi-ethnic, multi-racial, and multi-religious society. Freedoms afforded individuals from many different backgrounds are the very essence of our democracy. Children spend many hours in school during their development years. It is essential that we don't use that learning environment as a tool to impose our value systems on all children.

The concept of separation of church and state is fundamental to our system of government. State involvement in personal religion was one of the prime reasons our country was established. Our society must continue to debate the issues listed above, but in so doing should not ignore the primary purpose of educational institutions—to teach.

Our Nation Should Protect Our National Cultural Treasure and Promote the Financial Support of the Arts and the Humanities

Historically, primary support for the arts and the humanities has been from private sources. The federal tax laws should continue to promote charitable contributions which provide that support. However, policymakers should recognize that there are significant national treasures which require a direct federal commitment.

Access to museums, the arts, the humanities and the legacies of our past must never become only the province of the privileged few. The cost of protecting our heritage is quite high and there are many cases when private funding alone is insufficient to provide that support.

* * *

As noted before, the tone of the national debate on education and training is probably as important as the specific measures for reform. True reform occurs at the state and local level. However, the federal role has been, and should continue to be, to stimulate that reform where national concerns or needs are involved.

The job demands of the coming decades must be met by a skilled workforce in order to remain competitive in a world economy and to maintain a viable national defense. Current education trends and projected demographic trends suggest that the job will not be easy. The failure of the federal government to participate fully in reform endeavor would be a national tragedy.

Up Against the Wall: Religion and Politics in the United States

Alfred W. Tate

Americans find the question of the proper role of religion in politics a perennially perplexing one. One reason for this is the way in which these two ways of being and acting are inextricably related. The intimate connection between the "religious" and "political" dimensions of our lives has made discerning the distinction between the two difficult throughout history.

For Americans this difficulty is compounded by the peculiar disjunction between religion and politics institutionalized in the so-called "establishment clause" of the First Amendment. The unique experiment in governance the rejection of a national religion represents has left us without historical precedent for understanding the role of religion in the politics of the United States.

But we have placed ourselves at a further disadvantage. The terms in which any issue or question is put will in large measure determine the range of responses to it that are thought to be worth serious consideration, and nowhere has this proven more clear than in our ongoing national colloquy on what part, if any, religion should play in our system of governance. That is to say, the problems we are having in answering this question can be traced to the inadequacies of the language we have used to frame it. Almost immediately after the nation's founding, Americans began to debate the place of religion in their corporate life using language that obscured rather than clarified the issue.

The unlikely villain here is Thomas Jefferson. Writing in 1802 to the Danbury Baptist Association of Danbury, Connecticut, Jefferson described the effect of the First Amendment to have been one of "building a wall of separation between Church and State." The phrase is one of the most often quoted in American politics and the image it contains has almost totally captured our thinking on the question of religion and politics. Jefferson's choice of words, however, was an unhappy one for several reasons. First, the concepts of "Church" and "State" did not then and most certainly do not now adequately describe the American experience. As Paul Kauper puts it:

> Church-state terminology comes to us from Europe and recalls a background which is quite unlike the American scene. It had its origin in a time when the church was indeed a single monolithic Church and government power was centered in a single ruler. It is inadequate to describe the American situation because of both the multitude of churches in this country and the dispersion of governmental power among the federal government, the states, and the local communities.

Jefferson's use of the term "wall" is equally unfortunate. The reference is to a permanent barrier, set in place once and for all along a predetermined boundary. This, too, does not adequately describe what was and is the case here. A far more accurate image for the state of affairs in America is found in a 1832 letter from James Madison to the Reverend Jasper Adams in which he addressed the potential for confusion created by the First Amendment. He had to admit, Madison wrote,

> that it may not be easy, in every possible case, to trace the line of separation between the rights of religion and the Civil authority with such distinctness as to avoid collisions & doubts on unessential points.

The point is that in the United States there is no "Church" in the traditional sense, rather there are a myriad of "churches." By recent count, there are over 1000 organized religious groups in this country to which the label could be applied. Similarly, there is no "State" in the sense of a single seat of government, but a variety of "civil authorities" with overlapping constituencies and differing jurisdic-

tions and powers. In such a context, the term "line," one definition
of which is a path without width and of indeterminate length generated by two or more points, is much more helpful. It allows us, as
the historian Sidney Mead has argued, to see that the relationship
between "religion" and "Civil authority" is a close, dynamic and
indissoluble one. Further, the image enables us to appreciate that,
under our system of governance, this relationship and its boundary
must be refixed in each new situation in which the question of its
definition arises.

To see why Madison's language is preferable to Jefferson's and to
better understand what we have inherited in the "establishment
clause" of the First Amendment it will be necessary first to define
"religion" and "politics" and then to turn to an examination of what
is different about the way in which they are understood to be related
in this country.

"Religion" is the name given to the system of beliefs and practices
expressive of the faith in the ultimate meaning of existence common
to the members of a community. The Latin root of the word means
"to bind," and, as both a constellation of beliefs and the source of
the standards by which morality is measured, religion performs two
"binding" functions. First, in providing answers to the questions of
life's ultimate meaning and purpose it gives individuals their sense
of personal identity and worth. In this sense, religion creates an
awareness of being an integrated self that both transcends its needs
and desires and is more than the sum of its experiences. Second,
religion makes genuine and lasting community possible. It does so
because it is our recognition of the possession of this same selfhood
and personal worth by others that unites us as individuals into
groups whose purpose goes beyond simple physical survival to the
enhancement of the worth of this shared selfhood.

"Politics", on the other hand, is the art or science of government.
It is the name given to the institutions and activities which define,
structure and give order to the life of a particular group or community. It is derived from a Greek word meaning "city" or "state." The
term and its cognates can be used to refer to an explicitly or implicitly
incorporated community of whatever limited or extended sort, the
way in which such a community is organized and the process through
which it functions, as well as the specific things its members do in
gaining control of and administering it.

"Religion," the British statesman Edmund Burke maintained, "is
the basis of civil society." The German theologian Paul Tillich said

essentially the same thing when he wrote: "Religion is the substance of culture and culture the form of religion." Implicit in both statements is the truism that every political entity, every human group, no matter how large or small, no matter how formally or informally organized, is founded upon and takes its shape and direction from the shared religious beliefs of its members. Religion supplies the content for which politics may be said to provide the social structures.

To live in a genuine community, whether one as intimate as the family or as impersonal as that of the modern nation-state, requires individuals to subsume their self-interest under the greater good represented by the whole of which they are part. By supplying answers to the question of life's ultimate meaning and goal, religion defines this greater good and offers the inspiration for its attainment; in doing so it justifies the sacrifices of self-interest our life together requires and sanctions the restraints imposed by society when these sacrifices are not voluntarily made. Politics determines how the demands of communal life are to be distributed and enforced, as well as what punishment is to be exacted and how it is to be administered when these demands are not met.

The fact that a discussion of definitions and distinctions of this sort seems abstract and artificial is itself a symptom of the impossibility of finally separating religion and politics. And it is this intimate nature of their connection that makes distinguishing between religion and politics in any specific society at any one time very hard to do. For most countries, however, the question of the role of religion in politics never arises. For reasons peculiar to our history, for Americans it does so constantly. Why this is the case lies at the heart of the revolutionary experiment launched on this continent with the replacement of coercion with persuasion as the foundation of governance, and when viewed in the context of the whole of human history, the radical nature of this experiment is clear.

From time immemorial, the religious power that "bound" human beings into groups was assumed to flow from top down. Its source was God or the gods, and it passed through an individual or group of individuals who were themselves believed to be a god, or to have special relationship with the gods, and who therefore ruled by "divine right." The distinction between "sacred" and "secular" realms with which we are familiar was blurred or nonexistent, and, in such a context, "church" and "state" were simply different names for the same political reality. The chief or pharaoh, king or queen, was head of both. The practice of politics and of religion were indistinguishable. Individuals, by virtue of being citizens of the state, were members of the church. The teachings of the church were embodied in the laws of the state; heresy and treason were synonymous.

Two fundamental and mutually reinforcing assumptions were at work. One was that the state derived its authority from the moral sanction given it by the church, and that the cohesion and well-being of any society thus depended on the adherence by its members to a common, and by definition true, faith. The second was that the only way to guarantee this necessary adherence to this true faith was for the church to see the coercive power of the state to inculcate the teachings and maintain the purity of that faith.

If this symbiotic relationship were to break down, personal immorality and social chaos were believed to be the inevitable consequences. Thus, when Constantine unified the Roman Empire in 323 A.D., it was assumed by all that if it were to have one emperor, one law, and one citizenship for all free men, the Empire must have one religion. Constantine attributed his success in unifying the Empire to his having converted to the faith, and with his coming to power Christianity was transformed from the religion of a persecuted minority to the state religion of what was then the whole of the known western world.

In the subsequent 14 centuries, these basic assumptions went unchallenged, and their validity remained in large measure unquestioned during the Reformation's revolt against the Roman Catholic Church. Thus, when the religious wars which dissolved the vestiges of the Holy Roman Empire were concluded with the Peace of Westphalia in 1648, political stability in Europe was achieved primarily by recognizing the territorial claims of the rival Christian communions. While Catholicism remained the religion of France and Spain, Anglicanism held sway in England, Lutheranism dominated in most of the new German states and the Scandinavian countries, and Calvinism ruled in Switzerland, Scotland and the Low Countries.

Whatever their real relationship, we tend to live rigidly compartmentalized lives and view our political, religious and economic activities as taking place in quite different and separate spheres of life. Thus the religious motives which the heroes of the great age of exploration said provided the impetus for their expeditions are now regarded as window dressing to hide the avarice that really underlay their efforts. The distinctions we draw were not as clear at that time, however, and the propogation of the faith was inextricably bound up with the exploration and settlement of the New World, including what was to become the United States.

Proof of this is the way in which the operative assumptions of that age regarding the relation of religion and politics were brought to these shores. Not simply did their related theologies follow the various national flags as they made their way across the Atlantic. More tellingly, while many of the initial immigrants to America came specifically to escape religious persecution, few were willing to allow freedom of worship within the borders of the territory they claimed. The Anglicans settling in Virginia, the Dutch Reformed in New York, the Swedish Lutherans in Delaware and the Puritan Congregationalists in Massachusetts—most assumed that state-enforced religious uniformity would be transplanted from the Old World and perpetuated in the New.

Moreover, most took positive steps to ensure that was the case. In the Plymouth Colony, the Pilgrims—perhaps the most celebrated refugees from religious persecution to reach our shores—gave the right to vote only to those certified "orthodox in the fundamentals of religion," passed laws against Quakers and other "heretics," and made financial support of the church compulsory.

Of course, by "fundamentals of religion" each group had something specific—and different—in mind. The first Charter of Virginia, for example, provided that "the true word and service of God and Christian faith be preached, planted and used . . . according to the doctrine, rights, and religion now professed and established within our realm of England." Provision was also made in Virginia for the maintenance of church and clergy from public funds, and in 1612 laws were enacted threatening the impious with fines, whippings, "a bodkin thrust through (the) tongue," and even death. Such threats by our forebears were by no means empty, as four men and women learned when under the provisions of a similar Massachusetts law they were hung for the offense of being Quakers. Only in Rhode Island, founded and for the most part populated by refugees from religious persecution in Massachusetts, and in William Penn's Pennsylvania was religious freedom an essential element in the colony's governance.

In light of this history, the religious freedom inaugurated in the United States can be seen for the extraordinary innovation it was. The weight of thousands of years of tradition was overturned in the relatively brief span between 1661, when the last Quaker was hung on Boston Common, and November 3, 1791, when the First Amendment went into effect.

A number of factors combined to bring about this religious revolution. As a practical matter, the individuals assembled in Philadelphia recognized it was unavoidable. If there was to be a "United States" of America, there had to be religious freedom. So many different kinds of Protestant communions—not to mention Jews and Roman Catholics—were present in the Thirteen Colonies that, if a genuine union was to be forged, there was no choice. If the new nation was to continue to attract the immigrants it needed to grow and if that growth was not to result in the eventual balkanization of the continent, religious liberty had to be instituted in some form.

Two broad options presented themselves. One was toleration of the sort practiced in England, with an established church and legally "tolerated" dissenting sects. Favoring this option was its familiarity to the offshoots of Europe's state churches, which remained dominant in all but two of the colonies until after the Revolution. Further, this option did not totally overthrow the assumption that some vital connection existed between the maintenance of a state supported "orthodox" religion and social and political stability. The other choice was more radical—complete disestablishment and the institution of religious freedom.

Two complementary factors were major contributors to the selection of the latter of these options. One was the influence of developments taking place in eighteenth century political thinking, and the emerging notion that the only legitimate basis for civil government was the uncoerced consent of the governed.

Here the direction in which the religious power ordering communal life flowed was understood to be the reverse of what it had been thought to be. Instead of flowing from the top down, from the divine to the human, according to this new way of thinking this power was now conceived as moving from the bottom up, from "the people" to the rulers they choose to act as their deputies. The management of political affairs was now viewed as everyone's business because, according to John Locke, "God, who hath given the World to Men in common, hath also given them reason to make use of it to the best advantage of Life and Convenience." Here the religious revolution Luther signalled with his proclamation of the "priesthood of all believers" had found its parallel in a Lockean "kingship of all citizens."

The other major factor contributing to the institutionalizing of religious freedom in the United States was the pietistic character of religion on this side of the Atlantic. Pietism tended to view religion as centered on the individual's relationship with God and emphasized the centrality of the believer's conversion experience. This experience and the relationship it established was all important. The drawing of fine distinctions among the niceties of theological systems was looked on with suspicion, and little importance was given to the formal rituals expressing these distinctions. What people needed, a figure like Jonathan Edwards maintained, is to have "their hearts warmed, rather than their heads filled." Further, here the church was understood to be a voluntary association of individuals bound together by a similar inner experience of God's saving grace in their personal lives.

Waves of religious revivals swept the colonies from the 1730s through and beyond the time of the Revolution. These "awakenings" gave religion in America the distinctive character it retains to this day. They tended to inundate the sectarian differences existing between the various communions holding sway in different areas of the new country, underscoring pietism's lack of concern for doctrine and ritual while reinforcing its emphasis on the voluntary, consensual nature of human associations. All of this contributed to the creation of a climate congenial to religious freedom when the Constitutional Convention convened in Philadelphia.

But to assert such factors were important in the disestablishment of religion in the United States is by no means the same as saying this nation does not have the same religious basis Burke claimed for all civil society. The coming together in Philadelphia in 1787 "in Order to form a more perfect Union" was as much, if not more, of a leap of faith than any political act before or since.

The system of government devised by the Republic's founders to accommodate both the democratic ideal emergent in the political thought of the eighteenth century and the reality of the religious pluralism prevalent in the Thirteen Colonies is embodied in the Constitution and Bill of Rights. In these documents may be found the outlines of the very real and positive faith on which the experiment in government of, by and for the people Lincoln called "the last, best hope of earth" is based. While any statement of its essentials will be inevitably oversimple and reductive, the historian of religion in America Sidney Mead has identified four fundamental tenets of the faith on which our system rests.

The first is the existence of God. The God in whom the founders professed to believe is one of will and purpose. This God is the creator of heaven and earth, the guide and sustainer of history, and final judge of the actions of individuals. Men like Franklin, Washington, Jefferson and Madison lived close to and worked with the natural order. As farmers—and remarkably ingenious inventors—they were constantly performing practical experiments aimed at increasing their understanding of and ability to manipulate the world. They naturally assumed that there is order and meaning in the universe, discoverable, if only in part, by men and women, and that human action, although always tainted by selfishness and greed, can be made to conform to that order and meaning.

A second tenet of our founders' faith is belief in "the people." The authors of the Constitution and Bill of Rights are often accused, with some justification, of attempting to structure into these documents protections for the interests of the elite to which they belonged. The notion of "We the People" with which the Preamble to the Constitution begins, however, eludes definition in terms of such a limited reference. As it is explicated in the entire document and as it has come to be applied, albeit with inexcusable slowness, the concept points beyond its more immediate meaning of white male property owners to an understanding of "the people" that transcends all historical individuals and groups, and stands, rather, for the whole of human life understood as the finite medium or vehicle God uses to achieve His infinite purposes.

The voice of the people is thus the voice of God, although not in any simple or direct way. The radical monotheism of the Constitution conceives of God as an omniscient and omnipotent deity existing beyond all that is and for whom no individual or group, majority or minority, politician, preacher, church or sect, could claim to speak exclusively. This while at the same time maintaining that in the governance of human beings there is no higher court of appeal than to the will of "the people," that is, to the course of human history itself.

A third tenet of the faith our system is founded on is the belief that the will of the people can provide our surest clue to the will and purpose of God only when all channels of communication and expression are kept open and accessible to all. The Judeo-Christian basis for this belief is that tradition's insistence that the power of God to reveal His will is limitless and cannot either be restricted by human institutions or confined to certain forms.

In eighteenth century political theory this belief found expression in the premise that all men are created equal and possess—under God and thus by "nature"—what the Declaration of Independence called "unalienable rights." Implied is the notion that God's purposes for creation can only come to fruition if His creatures are free to exercise these rights and the responsibilities accompanying them. It is in this sense that the American theologian Lyman Beecher described the experiment the United States is embarked on as one of a "powerful nation in the full enjoyment of civil and religious liberty, where all the energies of man might find full scope and excitement, on purpose to show the world by one great successful experiment of what man is capable."

To this point it would be easy to mistake the founders for utopian visionaries, overconfident of the ultimate triumph of reason and secure in the conviction that all that was required for truth and goodness to triumph was the destruction of repressive political and religious institutions. To suppose they conceived the goal of the democratic process to be perfect harmony and unanimity, however, is to fail to appreciate the depth of their insight into human nature and the capacities for good and evil it embraces. Madison expressed this insight in the Fifty-fifth Federalist Paper: "As there is a degree of depravity in mankind which requires a certain degree of circumspection and distrust, so there are other qualities in human nature which justify a certain portion of esteem and confidence." Reinhold Niebuhr put it more succinctly when he wrote: "Man's capacity for justice makes democracy possible; but man's inclination to injustice makes democracy necessary."

Underlying sentiments such as these is the fourth tenet of the faith on which our system is founded: the acceptance of conflict as not only unavoidable, but as a necessary part of the democratic process. Jefferson pointed to this in his "Act for Establishing Religious Freedom" in Virginia when he wrote that he believed "that truth is great and will prevail if left to herself; that she is the proper and sufficient antagonist to error, and has nothing to fear from the conflict unless by human interposition disarmed of her natural weapon, free argument and debate; errors ceasing to be dangerous when it is permitted freely to contradict them."

Two corollaries follow from this notion that the free conflict of opinions is the heart of the democratic process. The first is that each individual has the responsibility to contend for the truth as he or she sees it. The concept of freedom at work here is not a negative one which holds that, since anyone's opinion is as good as anyone else's, all should be permitted free expression. Rather, it is the positive contention that the relative merits of differing position or opinions will only emerge if all are openly and candidly debated and compared. Also implied is the belief that no human response to any situation will be perfectly appropriate or fitting, and thus all can be improved by being submitted to this process.

The second corollary following from this belief in the centrality of conflict to the democratic process is that the conditions which make conflict possible must be preserved if that process is to continue to function. That is to say, in order to maintain the essential conflict itself, the government may find it necessary—as the servant of all the people—to use its power either to ensure the continued existence of a minority threatened with extinction at the hands of the majority, or to preserve the system itself from a minority which would disrupt its functioning.

The economic, political and religious rights of minorities must be protected, therefore, not simply because the majority on any issue may well be in the wrong, but also because unless the right to dissent is preserved, the rights of all are jeopardized. "In a free government the security for civil rights must be the same as that for religious rights," Madison wrote in the Fifty-first Federalist Paper. "It consists in the one case in the multiplicity of interests, and in the other in the multiplicity of sects." Madison's point is that protecting the rights— and thereby preserving the existence—of minorities is critical because doing so maintains the essential condition which makes the conflict of democracy possible: the constant presence of opposition. From this perspective, the system of checks and balances and the distribution of powers contained in the Constitution may be seen to be intended to ensure that the conflict that is democracy is both productive of creative compromise and protected from being extinguished by either an overzealous majority or a disruptive minority.

We take so much for granted the fact that the United States has no established church to place its imprimatur on public policy that we tend also to overlook the fact that this represents an experiment in governance unique in Western history. Further, overlooked in turn is the way in which the religious freedom we enjoy in this country was not simply the consequence of practical necessity, but equally the expression of a profound religious conviction. This conviction is the belief that the free and open conflict of ideas and ideals is the essence of democracy.

In obscuring the true relationship between religion and politics

Jefferson's talk of a "wall of separation between Church and State" has obscured the faith stance on which our system is founded and led many to believe that the expression of religious convictions should somehow be excluded from the political arena. The opposite is the case. Our response to the ultimate religious question of the meaning of human existence is inextricably linked to our response to the fundamental political question of how shall we order our life together to most fully realize that meaning. Any specific effort to address the latter will inevitably entail an equally specific answer to the former. Every serious political debate will thus ineluctably be finally resolvable to appeals to the authority of religious convictions.

The establishment clause does not prevent such appeals. What it prevents is the use of coercion in any form by any side in such debates. The problem the First Amendment confronts is contained in the fact that the authority religious convictions carry is absolute because the questions to which they are responses are ultimate ones. Thus possession of such convictions brings with it the temptation to claim that the use of any means are justified in their imposition. The Constitution resolves this problem by confronting the claims to absolute authority by specific religions with a claim of equally absolute authority of its own. This claim is that—no matter how firmly held the faith on which they are founded may be—the political responses religious convictions elicit are always human products and thus relative and fallible. Their imposition must therefore be only through the medium of persuasion in free and open debate and never through the use of coercive force, however subtle its application.

The First Amendment created something very different from a "wall." It has instead provided the occasion for determining in any specific political conflict whether the expression of religous convictions by the parties involved is persuasive, and therefore permitted, or coercive, and therefore "unconstitutional." This determination can only be made on the basis of the particular issues involved and the specific modes of argument used. The result has been something much better described in terms of Madison's "line," a line the course of which has been generated by past such determinations and the direction of which will depend upon the circumstances of future political debates.

The inclusion in the Constitution of the edict that "Congress shall make no law respecting an establishment of religion, or prohibiting the free exercise thereof," meant that for the first time a political community incorporated as one of its founding principles the recognition that the demands of good citizenship can be at odds with the demands of the individuals' conscience as formed by his or her religious faith. This can arise in any area of life at any time. It occurs, to cite an obvious example, when the government's mandate to provide for the common defense is interpreted by the majority at any one time to require means—conscription, for example—which run counter to the religious scruples of certain religious denominations or sects. Providing for what the Constitution calls "the common defense" is an inherent necessity for political communities. At the same time, it has also been seen as providing for the recognition of the sincerity of those who on religious grounds espouse pacifism and refuse to be drafted. In the United States, people who differ on this issue, as well as with regard to abortion, school prayer and many others, may all claim with equal justification to be good Americans.

This justification does not reside in a passive toleration. The genius in our system lies in its comprising a process by which such value conflicts and the inevitable appeal to religious absolutes they entail can be worked out. The achievement Lincoln said is ours to "nobly save or meanly lose" is a system in which the free competition of ideas can produce compromises which approximate justice.

Throughout our history the authors of the Constitution and Bill of Rights have been identified as "deists" and even attacked as "infidels" and betrayers of orthodox Christianity. Regarding such central figures as Franklin, Hamilton, Madison and Jefferson, the "deist" label in larger measure fits. To the degree the trinitarian creeds of the early church are taken as the standard, they were "unorthodox." Whatever the precise meaning of these terms and however applicable to specific individuals they might be, the charge is beside the point and fails to recognize what those who met in Philadelphia accomplished. Their accomplishment consisted of devising a government by law rather than men—including themselves—a system the processes of which even their own ideas could not capture. The revolution they effected was from a rule by coercion to a rule by persuasion, and they did it the only way it could have been done, by submitting themselves to that rule. They were democrats, not theocrats or self-proclaimed messiahs.

Similarly, the system of government they devised has been said to be "atheistic," "godless," and more recently attacked as "secular-humanist." It is none of these, but again such charges are beside the point. They confuse the faith stance of the individuals occupying the offices of the government, which may be representative of any of the many religious traditions represented in this country, with the democratic process itself, which is neutral to the idiosyncrasies and vagaries of these groups. The United States is a republic; whatever the pretentions of some, past and present, it is not the Kingdom of God on Earth.

Like every other body politic, ours is founded on faith. What sets ours apart is that it is founded on the belief that the power that binds us together as a nation flows from "the people." While the authors of the Constitution thus stood the traditional notion of the direction in which this power moves on its head, the two fundamental and reinforcing assumptions on which the older understanding was based remain operative for us. As has been true for all tribes and nations from time immemorial, our system of governance retains its authority over us as individuals only so long as we remain convinced of the essential "rightness" of the faith on which it is founded. Further, as has also been true for all peoples in all times and as most recently witnessed to by the pageantry surrounding the celebration of the bicentennial of the Constitution, the power inherent in our institutions of government is constantly being enlisted in the cause of inculcating this faith. The stakes are high. If and when this faith loses its ability to give meaning and direction to our lives—and in the process inspire in us the sacrifice of self-interest life in community requires—our society will begin to unravel. For us that unraveling will take the form of giving into the temptation to allow the ends we seek to dictate the means we use to achieve them.

Ours is not a secular system, but it is a de-sectarianized one. It is founded on the dual conviction that no individual or group of individuals speaks for God, and, at the same time, that under God truth and right are not matters ultimately decided by majority vote. It is this conviction—this faith—that obligates the majority to protect the right of the minority to be heard, however outrageous its claims, while at the same time requiring the minority to respect the integrity of the process to which its voice is essential. Without this faith, democracy will descend into demagogic mobocracy.

Our Common Goal:
Preserving Environmental Quality

Senator Robert Stafford

"The ravages committed by man subvert the relations and destroy the balance which nature had established . . . The Earth is fast becoming an unfit home for its noblest inhabitant, and another era of equal human crime and human improvidence . . . would reduce it to such a condition of impoverished productiveness, of shattered surface, of climactic excess, as to threaten the depravation, barbarism, and perhaps even extinction of the species."

George Perkins Marsh
MAN AND NATURE,
1864

Conservation of our natural environment surely is one of the noblest and wisest forms of human endeavor, since its goal is the preservation of the life-support system that sustains all the species of the planet Earth. The species with the most at stake, of course, is us.

George Perkins Marsh, a Vermont businessman, lawyer, scholar and politician, became known as the "fountainhead of the conservation movement" when he published his objections to the misuse of land he observed in Vermont, Europe and the Middle East early in the nineteenth century.

How even more ominous his warnings would have been had he

known how we would infect our planet's air, water and soil with chemicals and wastes in the Twentieth Century!

But that may have been too much to ask of even someone so brilliant and prescient as Marsh, for the changes have been so gradual and so subtle that even the best of our modern scientists have scarcely recognized the dangers until recently.

Evidence to help us understand how vast and how dangerous these changes may be is only now being accumulated by the scientists. But, already we know that we must deal with a past that demands review and with a future that defies easy solution.

On that score, it is important to examine what we are doing and where we are going. We have challenges to face and we have choices to make. The choices are more limited than they were a century ago, or even a decade ago. That means the challenges are greater.

If we are to have a livable environment in the future, we must all clearly understand how much we will have to depend upon each other to achieve that objective. What are our common goals in this quest?

Surely the most basic are these: safe and adequate supplies of food and water; safe and healthy housing and workplaces; disposal systems for liquid and solid wastes that perform adequately, and air quality that enhances, rather than diminishes, life.

In this nation, our own and previous generations have made significant gains in the effort to achieve these basic goals. But, while we clearly must protect the gains that have been made, we and our children and their children face environmental hazards far greater than those that have already been contained.

It may be worthwhile to review the past before examining our prospects for the future.

During this nation's period of new frontiers and apparently unlimited resources, there was little perception that we had to restrain the processes that were damaging and diminishing the air, the water and the land.

Fortunately, some voices are raised in warning against some of this early abuse of our resources. Among the political figures whose voices and actions were most effective, in addition to Marsh, were Thomas Jefferson, John Quincy Adams, Theodore Roosevelt and Franklin D. Roosevelt. Each advocated that government should not be a passive observer, but should be a participant in the preservation of the nation's environment.

Still, in the years of rapid development of technology and its many products, most Americans were content to enjoy the benefits of the good life, with little concern for the side effects of that technology.

There was only a suspicion, supported by scattered facts and nagging doubts, that a problem of major proportion was building up all around us. That process began to pick up momentum after World War II. A newly-aware public and Congress were stunned by the evidence.

There were few clean streams and lakes in the country. There were millions of scarred acres. Smoke from industrial plants was poisoning the land and its people. Invisible pollutants were causing damage—not just to crops and to property, but also to the health of Americans.

The nation took the scanty information that had been gathered and embarked upon a moderate course designed to reduce pollution where we could demonstrate a cause and effect relationship. For nearly a decade, we tried to achieve a cleaner environment by negotiation. By 1970, it was clear we had failed in that effort.

Environmental pollution got worse, not better. It attracted not only the attention of the politicians—but it also ignited the concern of the public. It was decided that deterioration of our environment was a national problem.

The federal government decided that our nation could no longer afford the pervasive destruction of natural resources. We decided we could not afford the billions of dollars of measurable losses that our national policy—or lack of policy—was costing.

As a result of the belated awareness of the damage we had been doing to the environment, the Congress decided to end its policy of benign neglect of the quality of our finite natural resources. It was also noted at this time that there was no naturally occurring force in our society that would protect the environment against the forces that had been insulting it.

Thus, it was decided that environmental security would require a federal interest to protect the public interest—indeed, to protect the species. Experience has clearly demonstrated the wisdom of that policy at the time, as well as the wisdom of continuation of that policy in the future.

The national decision to establish a federal interest on behalf of environmental protection resulted in the enactment of the Clean Air Act and the Clean Water Act of the 1970s. There are many who believe history will record that there have been few laws as important to human well-being as those two acts. They did not, of course, constitute the final solution to the problems they confronted. But the

Clean Air and Clean Water Acts stemmed, and even turned back, the tides of pollution that were sweeping across the nation.

No sooner had we completed our initial efforts to begin the long-term protection of the quality of our air and water when we were faced with another—a new and frightening—environmental emergency.

It seemed to many Americans at first that the problem of manmade poisonous chemicals burst upon us without warning in the late 1970s. But there had been plenty of warning, including these words from the 1975 Report of the Council on Environmental Quality (CEQ) regarding the new chemicals produced each year:

"The diversity of their use and the adverse effects already encountered from some make it increasingly probable that chemical contaminants in our environment have become a significant determinant of human health and life expectancy."

We soon learned that CEQ's warning, if anything, was understated. Americans faced a new environmental crisis. Love Canal and the Valley of the Drums and Midnight Dumpers were the early headline subjects that were soon matched across the nation. From the San Joaquin Valley to the Great Lakes to the Hudson and Shenandoah Rivers—each contaminated by manmade, poisonous chemicals—the grim circumstances spread across the nation.

Once again, a public that demanded action prompted the federal government to enact a chemical Superfund law in 1980 and to expand and extend that law in 1986. Once again, the law was the final solution to the problem, but once again it was a confirmation of a national policy that demanded a federal interest on behalf of environmental security.

This rather recent development—the demand by Americans for intervention by the federal government on behalf of environmental security—may result in a cooling off of the long love affair Americans have had with technology.

Society in America, as in other industrial nations, depends on technology and it is no longer possible to turn back the clock or the calendar to simpler days. The very standard of living and quality of life in America depend on the exploitation of science. This method of using our knowledge has given us advanced medical and health-care facilities; comprehensive communications and transportation systems; and a mind-boggling array of products that make our lives more exciting and more enjoyable. And, of course, our economy is based on our technology.

Up to now, the driving force behind our use of science and technology has been the generation of profits for entrepreneurs, inhibited only by the decisions of the marketplace and minimum government regulation designed to provide safety and preserve individual rights. But in recent years there has developed a growing concern over some of the unanticipated side effects of technological advancement—particularly in circumstances where those side effects threaten human health and the quality of life.

There are growing numbers of Americans, for instance, who seem to have reached agreement that uncritical approval of all applications of science and technology without concern for the side effects may not be in the best interest of mankind.

We have learned that when man disturbs an ecosystem with chemicals, he invites penalties to the system as a whole. Nuclear testing on Bikini Atoll raised radioactivity levels all over the world. It is an off-repeated truth that the use of DDT for malaria control resulted in the development of resistant strains of mosquitoes and caused increased concentrations of the chemical in other creatures until it was found even in penguins in Antarctica.

We are also learning that, for the first time in history, the extent of man's activities may be limited not by the scarcity of his resources, but by the problem of disposing of his wastes.

This growing awareness that economic deficits may dominate our current headlines, but ecological deficits will dominate our future, should encourage us to understand that we must reach a better balance between our luxuries and our necessities. We Americans will also have to understand that the quality of our future will depend to a great extent upon how well other inhabitants of this planet deal with their resources and environmental challenges.

Among the major environmental challenges Americans will have to deal with in the immediate future are:

• Enhancement of the quality of our air, both indoors and outdoors, and in the stratosphere as well as at ground level.
• Protection of our supplies of groundwater, in particular, as well as protection of other resources in general, from contamination by our waste matters and other substances.
• Safe management of radioactive materials and wastes, particularly those involved in the production of electric power and in the decommissioning of nuclear power plants.
• Conservation of tropical forests and biological diversity in other parts of the world.

Prudence clearly dictates that we alter our behavior in response to the urgings of world scientists who have warned that humanity is conducting a "giant experiment" with the future of the Earth—an experiment whose outcome cannot be predicted. It is no exaggeration to say that it is literally too late to halt some of the changes we have caused. Those changes will have to be endured. But it is not too late to soften the impact of some of those changes and, more importantly, to avoid others. To do so requires a resolve to end our short-term gratification at the expense of the environmental capital of our children.

There is still time to act, but our time and our options grow more limited. Indeed, a brief examination of some of our major environmental challenges suggests that the level of urgency is higher than all but a few appreciate.

OUR ATMOSPHERE

The Earth's atmosphere serves a dual role. First, it provides living organisms with the most vital of all nutrients—oxygen for animals and carbon dioxide for plants. Second, it shields all living organisms from the deadly radiation and cold of space. Evolved over millions of years, the chemistry which creates this enriching and protective medium is highly complex, involving literally hundreds of different and poorly understood chemical and physical reactions.

Pollutants and other chemicals disrupt these reactions and, in so doing, destabilize the atmosphere. Trapped inside the atmosphere in varying concentrations, these pollutants become poisons for plants and animals alike, altering the web of biological relationships through which one species of life sustains another thousands of miles away.

Man understands this web of chemical, biological and physical relationships so poorly that even the simplest of questions—such as how many miles a given pollutant will travel—cannot be answered with certainty. It is in large part because of this lack of knowledge that a preference for leaving things as they are must be the benchmark against which all actions must be measured. It is because even the smallest mistakes have vast impacts that we must learn to be more careful about our actions. In defense of the environment, every victory is temporary, every defeat permanent.

The volume of pollutants and chemicals poured into the atmosphere is staggering. In the United States alone, industrial and utility smokestacks force more than 22 million tons of sulphur dioxide into the air annually, a major cause of acid rain. A single tank of gasoline for the average American automobile produces roughly 300 pounds of carbon dioxide when consumed. And chlorofluorocarbons (CFCs) are produced at a rate of more than 700,000 metric tons a year. CFCs pack a double wallop because they not only destroy the protective ozone layer, but also cause global warming. They would continue to cause damage even if we were to stop using them immediately, because it takes CFCs between 65 and 110 years to be broken down in the atmosphere after they are released.

In any discussion of air pollutants, it is helpful to be reminded of the true nature of each of the pollutants. Oxides of nitrogen are growth stimulants. Oxidants are bleaches. Sulphur dioxide forms acids. Considered in this manner, there should be no surprise that the first signs of oxidant (more commonly known as "smog") damage to a tree is the bleaching of the needles, turning them a sickly yellow-green. In fact, this lower-level ozone is so effective at destroying organic matter that it is used by many cities to disinfect their drinking water supplies.

The real concern, of course, is not merely the overwhelming volume of these chemicals, but their nature and the extent of the damage they may cause.

Carbon dioxide (CO_2), the major "greenhouse" gas, is responsible for most of the projected global warming trend that scientists tell us may result in an average temperature increase around the world of between one and three degrees Centigrade. Such a change could turn the breadbaskets of the American Midwest, the Soviet Ukraine and Middle Europe into dustbowls. Also, glacial and ice cap melting could raise water levels that could cause vast changes—and vast damage—throughout the world.

Carbon monoxide (CO) is a localized air pollutant that displaces oxygen in human blood. Older persons, particularly those with heart conditions, are vulnerable to harm. Even more vulnerable are unborn babies who, denied oxygen in the womb, could suffer permanent brain damage.

Oxides of nitrogen (NO, NO_2 and N_2O) are rich in nutrients essential to trees and other plants. They stimulate growth, sometimes in the wrong seasons, which leaves plants vulnerable to early or late season frosts and other stresses. These oxides of nitrogen also react in the presence of sunlight with volatile organics (such as gasoline fumes) to form the lower-altitude ozone we call "smog." More recently, some have come to refer to "smog" as "smozone" to distinguish it from the "good" ozone in the stratosphere that shields the planet from ultraviolet radiation.

Smog damages human health, crops, trees and structures. At the end of 1987, the Environmental Protection Agency estimated that eighty million Americans were living in areas where ozone levels exceeded the legal limits set to protect public health.

Sulphur dioxide (SO_2) is created when sulphur contained in virtually all fossil fuels, but particularly in coal, is burned. It pours out of the smokestacks of electric utilities and other industries as a colorless gas and is a triple-threat pollutant because it transforms into three different chemicals as it hangs in the air for days. Sulphur dioxide causes lung damage and erodes building materials. At higher concentrations, it also kills trees and other vegetation. After a few hours, it becomes an extremely fine solid particle—sulphate. This particle is the perfect size to refract light and sharply reduce visibility. It is also the perfect size to elude the natural defenses of humans and to penetrate to the deepest, most sensitive regions of the lungs. Water in the air converts the sulphate into the third chemical—sulphuric acid. Trickling through soils, surging downstream in spring and summer rains, the acid unleashes a torrent of heavy metals—aluminum, cadmium, mercury and others. We don't know exactly how acid rain kills streams and lakes, but we do know it has killed thousands of them throughout the world, including many in our own Northeast and Midwest.

Chlorofluorocarbons (CFCs) have depleted the ozone layer of the entire planet, even though most of our attention has been directed at the "hole" that appears in the ozone layer over the Antarctic each Spring. Scientists tell us that one result of this depletion of the ozone layer that protects our entire globe may be an increase in fatal human skin cancers. There have been warnings of other dangers as well. For instance, the larvae of shellfish, the bottom of humanity's food chain, live in the top one-half centimeter of the ocean and ultraviolet light kills these shellfish. As luck would have it, most of these shellfish thrive in the upwellings of the polar oceans where the ozone shield is likely to be at its thinnest, thus offering the least protection against the deadly ultraviolet light.

Our atmospheric soup of contaminants contains a variety of contaminants—arsenic, benzene, cadmium, chlorine, fluoride iron, hydrocarbons, formaldehyde, mercury, manganese, nickel, sulphates, nitrates, ozone and lead, just to name some of the most common. It is estimated that harm caused by outdoor air pollution costs Americans $10 billion annually in health costs. This does not include the potentially greater cost of our tampering with the climate and weather-making mechanisms of the globe and the alteration of nature's regular cycle of life with these chemicals.

It is also well to remember that all air pollution does not remain in the air. It falls to Earth eventually. Even the pollutants that are gases are ensnared by the leaves of trees and by the earth as they pass over. Thus, soils near highways are frequently saturated with lead. Lakes, which we try to protect from waterborne pollution, are often contaminated with atmospheric chemicals. After two decades and billions of dollars of cleanup efforts, the Great Lakes are freer of regular water pollution than at any time in the last forty years. But the pollution of these magnificent lakes by toxic chemicals is increasing because pesticides and other chemicals evaporate from the land and then fall into the lakes. Other waters of our nation have been similarly contaminated.

We have recently been reminded by scientists that indoor air pollution may be a greater threat to health than pollution of outdoor air, particularly since most of us spend most of our time indoors. Naturally occurring radon gas, asbestos fibers in manmade products and exposure to tobacco smoke of others are deadly indoor pollutants that we are most aware of. There are also threats from the pollutants produced by the burning of gas for heating and cooking; by formaldehyde emitted from fabrics and building materials; from use of preservatives, solvents, cleaning compounds, glues, resins, disinfectants and hundreds of other products and materials used in our homes, offices, factories, cars, buses, trains and airplanes.

Some voluntary changes in behavior may result as we become more aware of the damage we are inflicting upon the global environment by our seemingly insatiable appetite for self-gratification. However, it is unrealistic to expect the inhabitants of this planet to voluntarily achieve the kinds of dramatic changes required to restore environmental balance on Earth. It is more likely that the government of the United States and the governments of other developed and developing nations will have to mandate the kind of actions needed to preserve our resources. To preserve and enhance our atmosphere, new government action is needed to:

• Reduce by at least half the volume of sulphur dioxide forced into our air each year. This goal can easily be achieved through the use of existing technology to clean up emissions from smokestacks of existing powerplants. Even more cost-effective emission control strategy includes conservation; switching to the use of cleaner fuel, and replacement of existing dirty powerplants with new and cleaner plants that are, at the same time, more efficient.

• Reduce emissions from motor vehicles. The United States leads the world in control of tailpipe emissions, but even American standards can be tightened to further reduce emissions of carbon monoxide, hydrocarbons, oxides of nitrogen and particulate matter through use of technology available at the present time.

• Eliminate the use and release of CFCs throughout the world. The United States government should continue to press for an international agreement to ban the use of CFCs. Our government can encourage approval of such an international pact by enacting legislation to ban in the United States the use of CFCs and of products made with CFCs. Substitute chemicals for CFCs are available for some uses, as are substitute processes and substitute products. A CFC ban by the United States would speed up the use of existing substitutes and the development of new substitutes.

• Reduce the production of carbon dioxide and nitrous oxide through reduction in the use of coal and oil by more efficient uses of those fuels and through conservation measures. A reduction in CFC releases will also slow the rate of climate changes.

• Educate citizens in the hazards posed by indoor air pollution to encourage efforts to filter and otherwise clean up the air in existing buildings and transportation vehicles and to alter our use of materials and technology in the future. Fuel used for home cooking and materials used in building construction, furnishings and maintenance should be selected for their impact on human health as well as for their durability and appearance.

GROUNDWATER PROTECTION

There is no way to place a value on clean water. It sustains our lives, provides our food and powers our industry. Americans have come to take for granted an inexpensive and inexhaustible supply of water that is healthy to drink; that tastes, looks and smells good; that doesn't damage our plumbing, and that is in such supply as to satisfy the needs of our agriculture and recreation as well. Our nation receives an average of 18,000 gallons of rainfall per person every day.

Two-thirds of that returns to the atmosphere through evaporation or transpiration. A little less than one-third reaches the oceans through surface or subsurface flow. We consume only about 2.5 per cent of our total daily supply.

These figures demonstrate that we Americans are in good shape as far as our water needs are concerned. We may not always have our water in the right place in the right amount of the right quality at the right time, but those requirements are met most of the time in this country. We have even done a reasonably good job of cleaning up our surface waters after we realized we were polluting them to the point of danger.

Still, we have recently noted a decline in the rate of that early progress of cleaning up our surface waters. And, we have just barely started to work on the big task of controlling the "nonpoint" sources of pollution. That's pollution originating from agricultural activities, urban storm water runoff, mining runoff, silverculture, atmospheric deposition and the products of individual wastewater systems we call septic tanks. In addition, the hazardous substances that leak from chemical dumpsites degrade surface water as well as groundwater.

Thus, if we are becoming aware of our inability to maintain our early progress in protecting the integrity of our surface waters, we had better become even more aware of the potential dangers to our groundwater, which contains more than fifty times the volume of our nation's surface waters. Groundwater is the major source of water for agriculture and industrial purposes and it provides more than half of the population of the United States with its drinking water. It is the primary source of drinking water for more than 95 per cent of rural Americans.

Groundwater constitutes 96 per cent of all the fresh water in the United States. We are using more of it each year. And, our groundwater is becoming contaminated. The most troublesome contaminants include organic solvents, such as trichloroethylene and benzene; gasoline, pesticides and soil fumigants; disease-causing organisms, and nitrates. Contamination comes from natural pollutants, human waste disposal facilities and other human activities, including spills and leaks.

The evidence is clear that contamination has been measured in virtually every part of our nation, but that less than one per cent of our underground water supply is polluted. Thus, we have become aware of the problem in time to do something about it. But we cannot ignore the danger because there is no assurance that we will be able to clean up our groundwater after it becomes polluted, as we have been able to do with our surface waters. It is clear that the best course is to protect the quality of our groundwater, rather than to hope we will be able to find a way to clean it up.

Once again a strong federal role will be required. To protect groundwater from further contamination, the federal government must ensure effective enforcement of existing laws designed to protect water quality. It is also vital that the federal government take the lead in working out with the states protection strategies and clear lines of enforcement actions. This lead by the federal government would establish two levels of protection of groundwater supplies.

• The first would require the best available technology to protect drinking water supply wellhead areas from infiltration of pollution from underground storage tanks, sewer lines, landfills and similar sources. Double liners would be among the kinds of best available technology required.

• The second level of protection would be provided through the development of federal guidance documents and standards that would be used by states to create state permit programs for such sources of groundwater contamination as sewer systems, landfills, surface impoundments of all types and some pesticide applications.

NUCLEAR WASTES

Nowhere has the world run up a greater environmental deficit than in the use of nuclear power, and the United States is at the head of the pack. After building about 100 power plants in this country—and nearly 350 around the world—over a span of forty years, we still have not found an acceptable way to dispose of nuclear reactors and their wastes and leftover fuel. In our global rush to build nuclear power plants before 1980, governments failed to require utilities to provide the methods and the money to manage their wastes and to decommission their plants at the end of their useful lives. The result is that those who have reaped the major benefits of this nuclear exploitation will turn over to their children—and, perhaps, to their children—the task and the cost of cleaning up the radioactive mess left behind.

The oldest commercial nuclear reactors are already nearing the end of their useful lives, and some plants have already been closed because of accidents or design faults. In the United States alone, dozens of tiny research and military reactors are no longer in use and at least four small commercial units are shut down and waiting for decommissioning. The Nuclear Regulatory Commission estimates that another 67 large commercial reactors will cease operations before the year 2010. Worldwide, more than twenty power reactors are already shut down; 63 more are likely to retire by the end of the century, and another 162 between 2000 and 2010 under current estimates.

Those prospects will challenge our waste managment capabilities on a scale unknown to us at present. We will be dealing with huge structures that have been irradiated at a time when there is no political consensus—here or abroad—on how to manage that waste. All of which suggests that we will add the wastes that our nuclear power plants will become to the wastes they have been producing all these years.

About 12,000 metric tons of commercial high-level wastes are already in storage in the United States and it is estimated that the total will quadruple by the end of the century. We store our spent fuel rods in water-filled basins at the sites of the operating plants and they will be an additional burden in the decommissioning process. Assurances from scientists that there are no technological problems to the safe management or radioactive waste are meaningless in the face of virtually unanimous political opposition to every technology proposed. Even if we were able to develop a consensus on a method of disposal, we are a long way from agreement on how to pay for plant shutdown. Decommissioning could cost as much as the original construction cost of each plant, with estimates ranging from $50 million to $3 billion per plant. No matter what the cost, it is clear it will be left for the coming generations to pay, since we have set very little aside for it up to now.

The nations of this world will eventually have to decommission about 500 nuclear power plants, more than 100 of them in this country. The governments of the world—including the United States government—had better get busy figuring out how to do it.

The stark reality is that there is no currently available method or technique for the decontamination and dismantlement of nuclear power plants that is acceptable to the American public. It is also true that the American public has refused to accept any proposal for the management of nuclear wastes. But we cannot continue to attempt to ignore the problem because it is too complex, too controversial and too costly. Nor can we continue to delay taking firm action on setting a national nuclear waste management strategy. There can be no complete decommissioning of nuclear power plants until we have established permanent disposal facilities for radioactive wastes. It is impossible to dismantle a reactor or the rest of a nuclear powerplant if there is nowhere to put the spent fuel and other radioactive material or machinery. It is clear that the responsibility to develop solutions rests with the federal governments that have encouraged and promoted our Nuclear Age. Our government and those of other nations must share information and experience gained through the decommissioning work at the small plants at Elk River, Minnesota, and Shippingport, Pennsylvania, as well as the knowledge gained at the damaged reactors at Three Mile Island and Chernobyl. Permanent nuclear waste disposal facilities must be established and firm and detailed guidelines and standards for that nuclear waste disposal strategy must be made available to the public as well as to the utility industry. Above all, public safety must be the prime consideration in this effort, and the temptation to save time and money by cutting corners must be resisted.

RAIN FORESTS

Scientists on both sides of the Iron Curtain have warned that almost all of the world's tropical forests will be destroyed in the next thirty years unless current trends are reversed. If that prediction is realized, one result could be death by starvation for up to one billion people in the tropics. In addition, destruction of the tropic forests could eventually alter global climate, create deserts and lead to the extinction of millions of species of plants and animals.

Tropical forests are being devastated by a clear-cutting pace of more than forty acres a minute to meet the food and fuel needs of the fastest-growing region of our globe. As the forests are cleared, the carbon dioxide once bound in the vegetation is released into the atmosphere, contributing to the "greenhouse" effect scientists tell us is gradually warming the Earth. Tropical forests erode easily and quickly become infertile, making reforestation difficult and leaving deserts behind. Also left behind, without support, are plant and animal life. It is estimated that up to ninety per cent of the thirty million species on Earth are contained in tropical forests.

Since all inhabitants of the globe will suffer from the consequences of continued destruction of tropical forests, it is clearly in the national

interests of the government of the United States and of other nations to act. What is needed is support for conservation projects that will demonstrate ways tropical nations can meet the food and fuel needs of their exploding populations without destroying their forest resources that sustain us all.

The hazards to our survival and to the survival of this planet as we know it are not limited to those few that have been already discussed. Poisonous chemicals—almost all of them manmade—of unknown consequences and unknown quantities are released into our environment each day. Most of these releases result from everyday, ordinary conduct. This conduct includes our use of pesticides; accidents ranging from the leaking of underground storage tanks to derailment of railroad tanker cars and the spills caused by tanker truck crashes. We continue to be endangered by the malevolent acts of man in cutting corners in the disposal of chemical wastes and other pollutants. Our nation continues to produce more waste than we can handle. Our landfills overflow and garbage barges roam the seas, seeking ports that will accept their rotting cargo. Our plastic cups and plates and cartons and our discarded glass bottles and metal cans litter our parks and streets and beaches and playgrounds.

We cannot continue on this course. The life-giving elements of our environment are being endangered by our activities. The challenge of the future is clear. And so is the choice.

Mankind is a family of fragile human beings, existing in a fragile environment. We live our lives and our hopes in a narrow band of sustenance, between a thin layer of earth and an even thinner film of ozone that protect us from the fiery core of the globe below and from the freezing and radiation of space above. If we are to survive under these marginal circumstances, we will have to continue to use the instrument we have created—our federal government—to defend our environmental security against the forces that threaten us all.

Towards a Stronger Majority Party: Let Independents Vote in the Primary

Roman Buhler

Political parties are today themselves at a crossroads. Weakened in recent years by demographic and technological changes, parties in general and the Republican Party in particular must find ways to restore their function as creators of lasting majority coalitions in American politics.

Several forces have contributed to a changing party structure in recent years. Political parties have become significantly weaker, and their influence has diminished. Precinct and patronage politics controlled by party organizations have been replaced with the media, big donors, and professional consultant-dominated politics. The advent of computerized direct mail in the 1970s has reduced the dependence of local candidates in urban areas on party organizations. Furthermore, increases in the social and economic mobility of the American electorate has reduced, but not eliminated, the traditional importance of inherited party registration and voting habits.

Political parties have also changed because interest groups focused on emotional, single-interest constituencies have increased. The civil rights movement, the environmental movement, the various anti-war and disarmament movements, the right-to-life movement and the so-called "Christian Right" movement have all had a significant impact on the American political scene. In many cases, these groups have been more able to motivate activists and donors than the party organizations themselves.

What this means is that party members interested in building a majority by appealing to the middle rather than by mobilizing the extremes, must ponder their strategy. I would argue that strengthening political parties is good for our political system and that only by reaching out can they strengthen themselves.

With proper leadership, parties can be mediating, rather than polarizing, influences on the political system. Properly articulated, the broad themes of a party, or a movement within a party, can be made appealing to activists and voters. And the necessity to articulate such a philosophy forces strategists to think of the general, as opposed to the special or regional interests.

There is no adequate replacement in sight for the parties as developers of political talent from the grassroots up to the level of candidacy. And no other institution in American politics allows the average citizen who is neither wealthy nor an elected official to participate with such effect on the governance of our country.

But strengthening a political party does not necessarily mean strengthening the ability of a few activists to discipline others on matters of ideological orthodoxy. Strengthening a party means recruiting more volunteers, raising more money, training better candidates, developing issues that appeal to a majority of voters, registering those voters to vote, turning them out on election day, and combining those elements to produce electoral majorities.

OPEN PRIMARIES

The problem for progressive Republicans in particular and for majority party builders in general is how to attract into the party a broad enough spectrum of participants to adopt the policies that will encourage winning candidates. An option with unique advantages is the opening of primaries to independent voters.

To build a majority party, Republicans must simply recruit more people. Most Republicans, especially progressive Republicans, talk a great deal about outreach, being "inclusive," and "broadening the base of our party." But how? The Golden Rule of politics is not merely "he who has the gold makes the rules," but perhaps more subtly "he who makes the rules gets the gold." Republicans do not

have the "gold," a legislative majority, so, as Butch Cassidy said, "let's discuss the rules."

If Republicans are serious about increasing participation in our party, here is an opportunity to bring millions of independent voters in at once, not just one at a time through individual changes of party registration. Independents who have participated in a party primary are much more likely to vote in November for a party candidate with whom they are familiar. This means one they have seen before on the ballot, especially at the local level where the candidates are seldom seen on television. Thus can Republicans develop more support and a better chance of winning general elections.

At the same time, Republican campaign resources can be more effectively directed towards vital swing independent voters starting in the primary election, rather than waiting until the general. This is especially significant in the urban and suburban legislative districts where targeted direct mail is more cost effective than broadcast media.

Typically, as the minority party in most areas, Republicans depend more on support from independent voters than do Democrats, who must simply unite their own voters to win.

Progressive Republicans potentially can appeal to independents who would greatly strengthen the progressive coalition which often reaches across party lines. And the Republican Party "regulars," who put winning ahead of ideology, left or right, can be reassured that the inclusion of independents will attract a large number of voters in the primary who will be more likely to support Republicans in November. These independent voters may also have an influence on the outcome of the primary. They will help nominate candidates who by virtue of their appeal to independent voters will be more likely to prevail in November.

The attention of independent votes in a primary could also reduce the pandering of candidates and campaign themes to narrow special interests within the party and encourage candidates to emphasize the same themes in the primary as they do in the general election. More than one Republican has been embarrassed by a position taken to win a primary only to regret it, or worse, contradict it in the general election.

There are, however, several reasons for some Republicans to be concerned about the inclusion of independents in the GOP primaries. Some Republicans fear a dilution of Republicans principles. What good, after all, is a GOP majority if the members are no longer

Republicans? Others will mention the red herring of raiding, the hypothetical concept of independents voters being secretly organized by members of another party for the purpose of invading the Republicans primary and nominating the weakest candidate.

Neither concern is cause for alarm. First, one must counter the arguments about the dilution of Republican principles with the realization that the Republican Party has absolutely no power if it does not elect legislators. And, though independents might pull the candidates slightly in one direction or another, the final result would be the increased likelihood of Republicans being elected. Second, the experience even of a pure open primary state like Washington, where not only independents but all voters are free to vote in any primary, indicates that raiding is not a significant problem.

Two states provide examples of why independents should be included in primaries. The first is Connecticut, where the debate over the inclusion of independents became a legal battle which resolved some questions and raised others. The second is California, where conditions are favorable for an experiment with open primaries.

A recent Supreme Court case between the State of Connecticut and the Republican Party of Connecticut illustrates that the question of whether independents will, or should, be allowed to vote in Republican primaries might not be purely a question of ideology. There are also some difficult legal questions.

In December, 1986, the U.S. Supreme Court, in the case of *Tashjian v. Republican Party of Connecticut*, gave political parties the right to allow independent voters to participate in the primaries which nominate the parties' candidates for office. In the past these rules were controlled by the State Legislature, which was often dominated by Democrats, and rarely by those interested in upsetting the status quo.

But now, because of the ruling in the *Tashjian* case, each state party organization has the right to allow voters who have not registered with any party to participate in primaries.

The *Tashjian* case originated in the dilemma faced by U.S. Senator Lowell Weicker, a progressive Republican from Connecticut. A fiercely independent Republican noted for his role on the Senate Watergate Committee, Weicker has never ceased to outrage conservative Republicans and to dismay organization Democrats, both of whom would like to replace him.

The Connecticut senator and his party allies resolved not to let this potential hazard become a reality. Their strategy was to change both the party rules and the law of Connecticut to allow independent voters to participate in Republican primaries. Connecticut has about 550,000 independent voters and fewer than half a million registered Republicans. Together independents and Republicans outnumber the state's approximately 700,000 Democrats. Broadening the Republican base in the primary made good sense to Weicker and his majority coalition allies.

Weicker first moved to consolidate his already considerable influence in the Connecticut GOP. He became one of the few progressive Republicans in federal office to succeed in this task. His effort has provided a model for others.

By September 1983 the reformers in the Connecticut Republican party were able to pass a motion calling for a state convention to consider altering the party's rules to allow independents to vote in the Republican primary. The convention was held and the rule was adopted in January 1984.

During the 1984 legislative session the Republicans in the Legislature sought to change the law but were blocked by Democratic majorities. In the November 1984 elections Republicans won a majority in both houses of the Legislature and passed legislation to allow independent voting. Democratic Governor William O'Neill, however, vetoed the legislation.

The Republican Party, meanwhile, had begun a lawsuit to overturn the state law on constitutional grounds. The defendant, Julia Tashjian, was the Democratic Secretary of State responsible for administering the election laws. The plaintiffs, in addition to the Republican Party of Connecticut, were Senator Weicker, progressive Republican Representatives Stewart B. McKinney and Nancy Johnson, and Connecticut GOP Chairman Thomas D'Amore, Jr.

After Republican Party victories at the District Court and Appeals Court levels, the case reached the U.S. Supreme Court and was argued in October 1986. The majority opinion, written by Justice Thurgood Marshall, overturned the law of the State of Connecticut in favor of the party rule. Marshall was joined in his opinion by Justices Brennan, White, Blackmun, and Powell.

The Court held that the right of free association guaranteed by the First and Fourteenth Amendments protected the right of the Connecticut Republican Party to determine limits of participation in party primaries. Marshall explained that, "[the] Party's attempt to broaden the base of public participation in and support for its activities is conduct undeniably central to the exercise of the right of association."

In handing down this ruling, the U.S. Supreme Court placed the initiative squarely with the political parties of the 50 states.

CALIFORNIA AND THE OPEN PRIMARY

The next issue to consider is the effect on and by the individual states as they consider opening their primaries. California could become a laboratory for the forging of a new direction for the Republican Party, just as it was in 1964 when Barry Goldwater's upset victory in the California primary signaled the ascendency of the conservative wing of the GOP. Both in terms of its national influence and because of the internal characteristics of its Republican Party, California is one state which lends itself to experimentation with open primaries.

Of particular significance is California's large and still growing share not only of the U.S. Congress, but of presidential nominating delegates. The reason is its winner-take-all presidential primary. California has been a swing state in internal Republican politics. This began under the stewardship of Earl Warren and his political successors, when California provided the key votes needed to nominate Dwight D. Eisenhower over the more conservative but perhaps less electable Robert Taft.

Warren was elected to office under a hybrid system of cross filing, which permits candidates to appear on the ballot of all voters in the primary, not just those of their own party. Cross filing was enacted by an earlier generation of progressive Republicans led by Governor Hiram Johnson, who later became Teddy Roosevelt's Bull Moose running mate in 1912.

Democrats, who took advantage of the 1958 recession and bitter infighting between conservative and moderate Republicans, won the governorship and legislative majorities. One of their first priorities was the replacement of cross filing with closed primaries. Perhaps it is no accident that Democrats since then have held nearly unbroken majorities in the California Legislature. This has been so during the years that Ronald Reagan served as governor as well as during the tenure of the even more popular current governor, Republican George Deukmejian.

But in the June 1964 California Republican presidential primary, a generation of moderate control of the national Republican Party was broken and Barry Goldwater defeated Nelson Rockefeller. Since that time California has been the home of the conservative wing of the Republican Party; in short, it has been Ronald Reagan's private preserve. The coalition of the Northeast, Midwest and California that dominated Republican politics in the Goldwater era has been replaced by a coalition of the South, Mountain States and California. The result has been to pull the party to the right.

But the addition of one million independent voters to the four million currently registered Republicans could have a significant impact on the state's politics and on the orientation of the state's Republican congressional delegation. The latter could also expand by at least five seats as a result of the 1990 census and reapportionment. Such a change could greatly affect national Republican politics.

Currently, California Republicans depend on independent and Democratic support to win elections. Republican registration in California is around 38%, Democratic registration is 50%, and most of the remainder are independent voters declining to state a party affiliation. Statewide and in marginal legislative districts Republicans are successful when they win 80% of the Republicans, 60% of the independents, and 30% of the Democrats. Without a strong majority of independents, Republicans lose.

The impact of a Republican decision to allow independents to cooperate in choosing a nominee will not be lost on the Democratic Party, where some leaders have already suggested that the party beat Republicans to the punch and open the Democratic Party to independents.

Should this occur, a significant increase in the number of independent voters could result. Swing voters in both parties would be free to choose their best opportunities from either party on election day by registering as independents.

Since more swing voters are Democrats than Republicans, Democrats could lose far more to reregistration than Republicans, perhaps making the GOP a majority party in California. Furthermore, should Democrats continue to freeze out independent voters, Republicans will have nearly as many voters participating in their primary as do Democrats. This could have serious consequences for Democratic local candidates running in marginal districts with substantial numbers of independents. Opening Republican primaries on the eve of reapportionment could prove to be the decisive element in winning Republican majorities in the Legislature and could result in further Republican gains through fair reapportionment.

MAJORITY BUILDING VS. ORTHODOXY

These developments in one state are only illustrative of the potential for dramatic changes in both parties across the nation. The outcome of the debate within the parties over the independent participation in the primary will provide an interesting barometer of the direction in which political parties seeking to strengthen themselves will go. How many will think in terms of majority building and how many will think in terms of orthodoxy?

The Supreme Court decision that set this process in motion is part of a larger trend in American constitutional law. That trend is toward giving political parties more freedom to govern their own affairs under the First Amendment "freedom of association" clause.

If progressives are to influence the debate that will now take place within the party over participation by independents, they cannot do so with words alone. Only through effective organizing within the party structures can progressives prevail in what are sure to be hotly contested internal state party votes on the rules changes that will allow independent participation.

Progressives can gain the initiative within party structures but rarely without new activists. To get them, progressives must refocus their agenda, just as they seek to refocus the party's agenda, on the recruitment of new people.

First, progressives must invest in youth. There is no easier place to recruit bright, highly motivated future leaders than in colleges and high schools. Time and money expended in these areas produce more leaders for the resources invested than most other forms of political recruitment.

Second, progressives must not fear to speak out for their agenda. The network of progressives will only grow if future members hear about their ideas and their work. The skilled compromiser who actually reaches a position of influence in the party organization and uses it for real change, often begins as a recruit motivated by the desire to speak out on a controversial issue.

Third, progressives must train themselves and their recruits for long term action inside political parties. The Saturday workshop and the weekend retreat build the group comraderie and the specific skills that make party coalitions possible. Parties, unlike candidates' coalitions, do not transform themselves overnight. But that means that party influence can be a lasting source of power. Parties reward persistence and consistency.

Notes on Contributors

James Leach is chairman of the Ripon Society and a member of Congress from Iowa. A graduate of Princeton University, Congressman Leach has been chairman of the Ripon Society since 1981. He was elected to the U.S. House of Representatives in 1976, and now serves on the Foreign Affairs Committee and the Banking, Housing and Urban Affairs Committee.

William McKenzie is editor of the *Ripon Forum*, and since 1986 has been executive director of the Ripon Society. A graduate of the University of Texas at Austin, Mr. McKenzie also holds a masters degree in political science from the University of Texas at Arlington. In 1980, he served as deputy research director for Representative John Anderson's presidential campaign.

Ambassador Elliot L. Richardson is a partner in the law firm of Milbank, Tweed, Hadley and McCloy. Mr. Richardson is a former Ambassador to the Law of the Sea Conference and to the Court of St. James's. From 1970–1977, he served as Secretary of Commerce, Secretary of Defense, Secretary of Health, Education and Welfare, and as Attorney General of the United States. From 1969–1970, Mr. Richardson was Undersecretary of State and from 1965–1967 he served as lieutenant governor of Massachusetts. He also served as Massachusetts attorney general from 1967–1969.

Senator Mark O. Hatfield has represented Oregon in the United States Senate since 1966, and prior to that he served two terms as governor of Oregon. Hatfield is the second-most senior Republican

151

in the Senate and the Ranking Republican on the Senate Appropriations Committee, which governs expenditures for all U.S. military
and foreign aid programs. Hatfield is also chairman of the Arms
Control and Foreign Policy Caucus, a bipartisan group of 132 House
and Senate members.

Senator Robert Stafford is the senior senator from Vermont and has
served in Congress since 1961. As chairman of the Senate Environment and Public Works Committee during the 97th, 98th and 99th
Congresses, Stafford presided over some of the most significant
achievements in environmental legislation since the 1970s. A former
prosecutor and World War II veteran, Stafford has also served Vermont as governor and member of Congress.

Steven B. Klinsky is a general partner of Forstmann Little & Company, a private New York merchant bank. He studied economics and
philosophy at the University of Michigan, graduating magna cum
laude and subsequently earning a law degree with honors from
Harvard Law School and a masters in business administration from
Harvard Business School. He is a member of the editorial board of
the *Ripon Forum* and a member of the National Governing Board of
the Ripon Society.

Donald T. Bliss, Jr. is a partner in the Washington, D.C. office of the
law firm O'Melveny and Myers. A graduate of Harvard University
and Harvard Law School, Mr. Bliss served as general counsel to the
Department of Transportation from 1974 until 1977. Mr. Bliss also
served as assistant to the Secretary of Health, Education and Welfare
from 1969 until 1973. He is now on the Washington Lawyers' Committee for Civil Rights.

William C. Clohan, Jr. is an attorney and partner in the Washington,
D.C. law firm of Clohan, Adams and Dean. Prior to joining the law
firm, he served as Undersecretary in the U.S. Department of Educa-
tion. Mr. Clohan has also served as Republican Counsel to the
Education and Labor Committee of the United States House of
Representatives.

Representative Nancy L. Johnson is a member of Congress from
Connecticut. Congresswoman Johnson was elected in 1982 and serves
on the House Select Committee on Children, Youth and Families. She
is the author of two major childcare proposals, the Child Care Act of
1987 and the Child Care Services Improvement Act of 1988. She was
a Connecticut state senator from 1976–1982.

Representative Bill Green is a member of Congress from New York City. Representative Green was elected to the U.S. House of Representatives in 1978 and is now the Ranking Republican on the House Appropriations Subcommittee on Housing and Urban Development and Independent Agencies. Mr. Green is also chairman of MODRN-PAC, a political action committee designed to assist moderate Republican officeseekers, and he is a member of the Congressional Caucus for Women's Issues.

Alfred W. Tate is a member of the *Ripon Forum* editorial board and an administrative assistant to Representative Jim Leach. Mr. Tate is a graduate of the Naval Academy and Union Theological Seminary in New York City. A Vietnam veteran, Mr. Tate also pursued graduate studies in religion at Harvard University.

Roman C. Buhler is an attorney in Los Angeles, California. Mr. Buhler is a graduate of Stanford University and the University of Southern California Law School. A longtime Republican activist, Mr. Buhler has managed several GOP local and legislative campaigns.